Church people in the United States of America, more than in any other nation, commonly shift their membership from one communion of the church to another, Bishop Dun points out. They do this for reasons of convenience, or marriage, or because they prefer another minister. The real differences between denominations are known to few, yet the essential unity of all believers in Christ is not understood either, and so the much-discussed united church does not come much nearer in the lives of the people.

Here is a book to help everyone understand—perhaps for the first time—both unity and difference in American church life. It will give substance and vitality to the slumbering will for church union. The book will draw interest from members of every communion because of its two important qualities: realism and idealism. Bishop Dun is realistic in recognizing that there are real differences between denominations which hinder union; he is idealistic in his faith and vision that the spirit of God can in time overcome these obstacles.

The church, in Bishop Dun's definition, is a <u>community for the worship of</u> God, an organism with both a soul and a body. He points out that while this description may be generally recognized, the various American denominations have three principal concepts: There is, first, the "catholic" idea which conceives the church as the *work* of God. Then there is a "classic" Protestant viewpoint which finds its authority for the church in the *word* of God. Finally there are the Protestant denominations which view the church primarily as a voluntary fellowship of those possessed of the *spirit* of God. These various viewpoints can be reconciled, he is convinced, within various frameworks and through the use of certain organizational devices which he describes in detail. The United Church to come, he says, may and must give room for all three concepts.

The book inaugurates a series on the general subject of Christian unity and much of it formed the subject matter of lectures delivered at the Disciples Divinity House at the University of Chicago. The lectures, to be known as the Hoover Lectures on Christian Unity, were endowed by the late William Henry Hoover.

The Author: ANGUS DUN has long been identified with thought and work for church unity. When the World Conference on Faith and Order convened in Edinburgh in 1937, he was asked to prepare a volume on varying conceptions of church unity, which had wide reading. He is the author of *The King's Cross, We Believe* and *Not By Bread Alone*. Since 1944 he has been the Bishop of Washington of the Protestant Episcopal Church.

THE WILLIAM HENRY HOOVER LECTURESHIP
ON CHRISTIAN UNITY

THE DISCIPLES DIVINITY HOUSE OF THE
UNIVERSITY OF CHICAGO

The William Henry Hoover Lectureship on Christian Unity was established by the Disciples Divinity House at the University of Chicago in 1945. Resources for the Lectureship are a Trust Fund established in the amount of Fifty Thousand Dollars some years prior to his death by Mr. W. H. Hoover, of North Canton, Ohio. The purpose of the fund was designated as the promotion of Christian unity, a cause for which Mr. Hoover demonstrated a lifelong interest. In the past the Fund had been used for initiating publications, notably periodicals which have since become well established. With the successful launching of these enterprises it was decided that the cause of Christian unity could best be served by establishing at a major university center a lectureship on Christian unity, no such lectureship having yet come into existence. The Disciples Divinity House of the University of Chicago was asked to accept Mr. Hoover's Trust for the purposes of sponsoring a lectureship on Christian unity.

The intention of those establishing the Lectureship is that each lecturer shall be a distinguished Christian churchman of this or some other country, whose experience, research and knowledge eminently qualify him to discuss the problem of Christian unity and to make a positive contribution toward closer co-operation of the many Christian denominations and the ultimate unity of the church of Christ.

A series of lectures is normally to be given annually and to be published as the Hoover Lectures.

THE WILLIAM HENRY HOOVER LECTURESHIP
ON CHRISTIAN UNITY

Inaugural Series

PROSPECTING FOR A UNITED CHURCH
By
The Rt. Rev. Angus Dun, D.D.

Prospecting for a United Church

By
ANGUS DUN

New York
Harper & Brothers, Publishers

PROSPECTING FOR A UNITED CHURCH

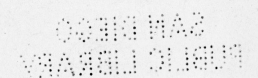

DEDICATED

TO THE FACULTY AND STUDENTS
OF THE EPISCOPAL THEOLOGICAL SCHOOL
IN CAMBRIDGE, MASSACHUSETTS
WITH WHOM I SHARED TWENTY-FOUR
HAPPY YEARS

CONTENTS

INTRODUCTION xi

I. THE WITNESS OF THE MANY CHURCHES TO THE
ONE CHURCH 1

II. THE WILL FOR UNITY 16

III. THE CHURCH AS BODY AND SPIRIT 29

IV. HOW THE CHURCHES THINK OF THE CHURCH: An
Essay in Understanding 44

   1. The "Catholic" Idea 44

V. HOW THE CHURCHES THINK OF THE CHURCH . . 60

   2. The Classical Protestant Idea 60

VI. HOW THE CHURCHES THINK OF THE CHURCH . . 75

   3. The Fellowship of the Spirit or the Community
of the Perfect Way 75

VII. PROSPECTING FOR A UNITED CHURCH 94

INDEX 111

CONTENTS

Introduction xi

I. *The Ideals of the Ideal Commonwealth* 1

II. *The Wisdom of God* 16

III. . . . .

IV. . . . .

V. . . . .

VI. . . . .

VII. . . . .

VIII. . . . .

INTRODUCTION

It has been a great responsibility as well as a great honor to inaugurate the Hoover Lectures on Christian Unity under the auspices of the Disciples Divinity House in Chicago. All who share the concern to which this lectureship is devoted must rejoice in the vision of Mr. William Henry Hoover, a loyal layman of the Disciples Church, whose generous gift made possible this foundation.

In the preparation of these lectures I have sought to write, not for the learned few but for the average minister and for the thoughtful lay members of our many churches. I can only hope that in so doing I shall not offend the learned few by too great folly. Inevitably, I have written as one standing in the American scene and looking out on the wider world scene from that standpoint. Inevitably too, I cannot escape the limitations of my own church setting, even though I have sought to transcend these limitations in imaginative sympathy. Above all, I have endeavored to write in charity, since he who speaks of the Church without charity speaks falsely.

The only apostolic succession I shall claim in this connection is that implied in the confession that I know I have not attained, but press towards the mark of our unity in Christ.

I am grateful for the kindness shown me by Dr. Charles Clayton Morrison, by Dean W. Barnett Blakemore of the Disciples Divinity House, and by many others during my visit to Chicago for the delivery of the lectures, of which this little volume is an expansion. I am indebted to my friends, the Rev. Professor Sherman E. Johnson of the Episcopal Theological School in Cambridge, Massachusetts, and the Rev. Canon Theodore O. Wedel of Washington Cathedral, for their generosity in reading the manuscript and giving helpful suggestions.

ANGUS DUN

March 1, 1948.

CHAPTER I

The Witness of the Many Churches
to the One Church

All of us meet with that distinctive reality we call "church" in terms of the local congregation of worshiping people into which our own lives have in varying measure been taken. We do not begin by analyzing it. Few ever analyze it very much. It is simply given. It is distinct from other associations or memberships into which we enter by inheritance or by choice. It is not the same as family or community or nation or club.

In it we gather with others, and commonly we cease for a time to talk with one another. One who is variously called our minister, our pastor, our priest or our rector, bids us remember that there is Another who is with us, and to be silent in that Presence. Or he begins straightway to speak to One who is not seen among us. Or he turns quite away from us to address this mysterious Other, with reference to whom all that takes place here seems chiefly to be concerned. Ancient Scriptures are read to us in a tone of special solemnity. They speak of God, and of One who bears the name of Christ, and of the Spirit; of who God is and what he has done among men; of commandments he has given; of One who came among us and died for us and rose again. They speak often of the people of God, of the disciples, of the Kingdom, of faith, of eternal life, of heaven.

We are bidden to stand and sing in words that speak of all these things and that are again commonly directed to this Other whose name is God. We are instructed to bow our heads or kneel while our

leader speaks to God in our name, or we join in saying "Our Father."
Or perhaps bread and wine are placed in hushed silence upon a
table or an altar, and after prayers and readings this bread and wine
are brought to us or we are summoned to go forward. And then the
words, "Take, eat," are spoken. Plainly this is no ordinary meal. It
is the Lord's Supper, Holy Communion, Eucharist.

There is much else that enters into our experience of church, but
let this suffice for now.

Surely, for the majority of us, the identity of the local church into
whose life we were first taken up was the result of unchosen circumstances. It was determined for us by the allegiance of our
parents or of one parent. It is like family membership in that respect,
though in the case of church we are commonly asked in youth or
greater maturity to make our own what is ours by unchosen inheritance. Most Americans, most men everywhere, who are actively
connected with a church belong to the allegiance of their inheritance. Very many have moved from the place of their birth and
childhood, but having grown up Roman Catholics or Presbyterians
or Methodists they have identified themselves with a local church
of their inherited membership in the place where they live.

This is not to deny that in the United States, to an extent probably
greater than in any other part of the world, many people have
shifted from a communion of one name to that of another, because
of marriage or convenience or the appeal of a particular minister,
without much sense of having taken a radical step. This is one of
the distinctive features of our American church life. A very few in
relation to the total membership of the churches have found a new
allegiance in mature life as a result of a deep conviction and with
the belief that they have now moved from false church to true
church, or at least to truer church. The changes of church allegiance
to which we are most likely to apply the term "conversion" are those
from a central "Protestant" body to a "Catholic" body on the ecclesiastical "right," or from a settled, respectable "Protestant" body
to a more enthusiastic evangelical group on the ecclesiastical "left."

However we come to membership, whether by childhood nurture

made our own in youthful decision, or by unchosen influences, or by deliberate choice in mature years, our actual concrete experience of church is found in the local congregation. Its ways of worship and manner of prayer have become our ways; the teaching we receive there defines for us the content of church teaching; its ministry is our ministry; its activities are church work for us; whatever its richness or limitations, we come to share in them.

While one cannot enter into a living experience of church without sharing in some local, actual manifestation of it, few stop there even as regards their conscious experience. We normally come to realize that our local congregation is tied in with a larger life. There are other churches with the same name, other Baptist churches or Episcopal churches or Roman Catholic churches. They are "our kind," ecclesiastically speaking. Of course the Episcopalians on Third street may feel that the Presbyterians on Main street are more "their kind," socially speaking; but church-wise they cannot deny that the little Episcopal chapel across the tracks *is* their kind.

How our local church is related to the other churches of our kind varies according to the kind. Generally their ways are our ways. We have never visited most of them or met the members face to face, any more than the people of Connecticut have met the people of Indiana; but as the people of Connecticut know that the people of Indiana are "part of the Union," fellow citizens of one nation, sharers together of common memories, making history together as one people, so we come to think and feel toward the other churches of our connection. They are relations, perhaps poor relations or rich ones. We may take pride that there are so many of us. Or, since we seem given to taking pride on *some* score, we may rejoice that though small we are select.

We go to meet another company of our kind as we go to another household of our family, with an expectancy of special welcome or even of special privilege, and of finding that we have much in common. Probably they use a book of hymns known to us. Perhaps they use a book of prayers which is as truly theirs as ours. It may be, as in the Episcopal Church, that there moves among the local congregations of our kind a chief pastor who is recognized and set apart to have a care for all the people of our kind in a wide area. We may learn that our minister, our bishop, and lay representatives of our local church meet together from time to time to take counsel for our wider common life. We expect to make common cause with other churches tied in with ours in many ways. We know that our gifts of money or of services are asked not simply to sustain the life of our own local church, but to build and sustain other churches of our kind in other parts of our own country or in far places.

In all these ways we come to realize that to belong to church is to have a part in something more far-reaching than our local congregations. That wider society we may call our "denomination" or our "communion" or our "church." And whether we are aware of it or not, it is plain that our local church is what it is because it is a part of this greater community of shared life. Whether by law or by those tenacious group habits we call custom, our ways of worship, our beliefs, the character of our ministry, the ways we are organized and governed come to us in large measure from the larger society of which we are a part.

That which bears the name of church among us, and which manifests the marks by which we commonly identify a church, is certainly not limited to churches of our kind. Unless we live in a very small community, there are other local congregations of other kinds living and praying and working alongside of us. We know them for the most part from the outside only, but we know that what goes on in their houses of prayer is in many ways quite recognizably like what goes on in our own.

I started to write this in a little hill village in New England. On the green stands a single white meetinghouse—the Union Evangelical Church—of somewhat tenuous "Congregational" connections. Near by is a community house that was once a Methodist church, and a red barn that once was a Baptist church, relics of the years before industry in the valleys and western farming sucked the population out of those hills. Most of the year-round residents of this community who are church people are members of this one church. There are summer visitors of other communions who as we say "attend it" during their holidays. Is this their church or isn't it? And there are Roman Catholics in the community who go to mass in a neighboring village. Plainly the "Union Evangelical Church" is not their church. Are both churches truly Church?

In the city of Washington, D.C., where I now live, the church directory lists 232 churches. They are grouped together according to their kinds: 32 Roman Catholic, 41 Methodist, 38 Episcopal, 24 Presbyterian, 38 Baptist, 7 Congregational, 7 Disciples, 21 Lutheran, 4 Orthodox, 5 Adventist, 1 Unitarian, 2 United Brethren, 3 Evangelical and Reformed, and so on.

That is probably fairly typical of the great cities of the United States, save as the distribution among the several group varies much in the different parts of the country. Are all these churches truly Church? The common man says that they are. But he takes an "outside" view. Would we find the answers more uncertain and unclear the farther we penetrated inside?

Without pressing the question now, we can recognize that the more widely we look, the more churches we find. In the United States alone there are some two hundred "religious bodies," to use the most neutral covering name. Almost all of them are in broadest terms Christian groups. Forty-eight bodies, each with fifty thousand or more reported members, account for 97 per cent of all the formally church-connected people in the United States. Among these larger bodies there are of course many denominations which most of us know at least by name. But even among these larger bodies there are those whose official names would have no intelligible associations for the great majority of American Christians. That is no condemnation of these less widely known groups; it simply reveals how largely our Christian communions are strangers to one another. We Christians are like a family that has lost track of its relatives, even of the names they have come by in the changes and chances of time.

Inevitably this sense of distance and this fading of the consciousness of relationship increase as we move through enlarging circles out into the world scene. We know that there are churches in every major area of our world, in Europe, Asia, Africa, India, South America, the Near East, the islands of the Pacific. Those who are members of the great church families know that their own kinds are to be found in the other lands. No American Roman Catholic can fail to realize that he belongs to a world-embracing society. He does not easily forget the pope, and the pope is a reminder of that fact. Few Episcopalians can be wholly unaware that they are sharers in a larger community of faith and worship, which is known as the anglican communion, and that a common inheritance from the mother Church of England binds them to all the sister churches of that communion in Canada, Australia, South Africa, and to the younger churches that have stemmed from that common life in India, China, Japan. American Presbyterianism has many ties with Scotland and with the far-spreading family of Reformed churches in Holland, France, Switzerland, and the English-speaking world.

Few could be expected to know even by name all the churches in the world. Even an approximation to such comprehensive knowledge is possible only for a few specialists. But we can know by name at least the main church families or church types which include by far the larger part of all the professing Christians in the world. They are the Roman Catholic, the Orthodox, the Anglican, the Lutheran, the Presbyterian and Reformed, the Methodist, the Congregationalist, the Baptist, the Disciples, the United churches (which have been formed by the union of previously divided denominations). Most of these church families, with the major exception of the Roman Catholic, are subdivided into many self-governing or otherwise separated parts, by nationality or race or other causes.

The major church families and their subdivisions differ from one another in many ways and degrees. Some are very much alike. Some differ greatly: they differ in their ways of worship, in the sacraments or ordinances they practice and in the place they give to them. They differ in the teachings they believe most necessary; as to where they find the standard for true belief; in the creeds or confessions of faith they use and how they use them. They differ in the way their churches are related to the state; in their attitudes to the world around them; in what they think their members most certainly should do or most certainly should not do. They differ in their conditions of membership and in the kinds of ministers they have and how they set them apart. They differ in the way their churches are organized or governed, and they differ in what is related to all of these, in what they think about the Church and what they consider essential to its being or well-being.

These churches not only differ; they are divided. To be different is not the same as to be divided; nor is likeness a guarantee of unity. Two men or two communities of men may have great likenesses, deep things in common, and be utterly divided because they have never met; there is nothing to make them conscious of each other, no traffic or communication between them, no overarching ties. Community, certainly communion, requires communication.

On the other hand, differences may be held within unity, depending on the degree or character of the differences and on the strength of the uniting forces. Marriage is by nature a union of differences. Two brothers may differ greatly and live as brothers in one household. There is no congregation of Christian people and there are no denominations which do not include many differences of opinion, temperament, experience. It has frequently been observed that many of the differences which supposedly separate Christian communions cut through existing denominations. All of which is not to deny that differences among men and groups of men are a chief cause of divisions among men.

Division among the churches manifests itself in many forms and degrees. Between some of them there is enmity, sometimes open, sometimes guarded or suppressed. They think and occasionally say hard things about one another. They would gladly see one another destroyed. Between others there is great distance, if not enmity; they have no dealings with one another, no traffic or exchanges. Some of these churches give one another a measure of recognition, have what we may call a bowing acquaintance, and yet go their own ways without taking counsel with one another. Still others have a deep sense of kinship. They view each other as allies. They work together and seek to help one another. Some are so close that it is hard to understand why they are apart at all.

Such, in their more superficial aspects, are the churches as we meet with them. The presence in our one world of the many, divided churches is so established a fact that most professing Christian people take it for granted. They have known nothing else. Their fathers and grandfathers before them knew nothing else. Yet there is that in all the churches which stands in contradiction to their plurality and divisions. They carry in their divided life that which brings them under judgment. Being many and divided, they all speak of THE CHURCH in the singular. Many of them treasure and use ancient creeds in which they constantly reaffirm, "I believe in the holy, catholic Church" or "one catholic and apostolic Church." They like to sing, "The Church's one foundation is Jesus Christ her Lord"; "Elect from every nation, yet one o'er all the earth"; "We are not divided, all one body we"; "We thank thee that thy Church unsleeping, while earth rolls onward into light, through all the world her watch is keeping, and rests not now by day or night"; "O blest Communion, fellowship divine, we feebly struggle, they in glory shine; yet all are one in thee, for all are thine."

We are tempted to cynical humor to escape the judgment of our own so widely shared utterances. Yet whatever their merit as poetry, these are the veritable utterances of Christian enthusiasm, of that enthusiasm which is a fruit of the Spirit. What is the Church whose "one foundation is Jesus Christ her Lord? . . . one o'er all the earth"? Who are the "we" who are "not divided, all one body"? Plainly, something more is meant than the present congregation that joins in the singing. Is the Church which is here spoken of and rejoiced in, the Methodist Church or the Episcopal Church or the Lutheran Church?

Multitudes of quite simple Christians have experienced in the singing of these hymns a sense of being part of something vastly greater than their local congregation or their denomination. And the meaning of their own little lives has been enlarged by this realization. There are few communities bearing the Christian name which are so earth-bound, or so shut up in the present and the immediate, that they do not at times express their consciousness of being knit into fellowship with the saints of the past and the saints in heaven. Whatever terms they use, they find in their deepest this-world and local expression of fellowship a sacramental fore-shadowing of something transcendent and heavenly. Nor do they readily divide heaven or the eternal Kingdom into denominational compartments.

The churches constantly confess the Church. As we look back into history, we see that each of the churches set out to be *the* Church, or a movement of recovery and reform within *the* Church. Only by a kind of tragic inadvertence did they become divided from that beyond themselves which they recognized as true Church. Each of them now claims to be either the one Church or a part of it. By the inner logic of their own life, they can do no other. Wherever each of them finds Church most unmistakably present, it struggles to maintain unity there, and views division as a scandal and a defeat. Every congregation struggles, sometimes against heavy odds, to maintain its unity. So does every denomination. There is that in the inescapable meaning of Church which cries out for unity. Indeed, it is just the tenacious attachment of each denomination to its own hardwon unity which often rises up to block movements for a closer association or union with another body that seems alien to it. The churches behave like families when one of their number proposes marriage into another family. They see their precious unity threatened by the wider relationship. And this unity which they seek to guard and perpetuate is not simply with their own present, but with their own past.

If all these churches have nearer memories of nothing save division, if they have their distinct and separating memories—Methodist memories, Baptist memories, Anglican memories—all have shared memories of a common origin and inheritance. Every

Christian body claims, in its own way, to be a true and legitimate descendant from a common life. All these divided churches guard and seek to hand on as their most treasured memories those which were gathered so long ago in the New Testament and before that in the Old Testament.

They all, quite literally, live on and by these memories, even as a family or a nation lives on and by its memories. What they read in their shared Scriptures, they understand not simply as spoken to and of the people of God in another time but as spoken to themselves. Out of these shared Scriptures they hear One whom they all acknowledge as their Lord, saying to them tenderly, "Fear not, little flock; for it is your Father's good pleasure to give you the Kingdom"; or again, "One is your Master and all ye are brethren"; and again, "Ye"—ye together in the common life into which I have called you—"are the light of the world and the salt of the earth."

All have treasured as the passionate prayer of their Lord for them the petition that "there shall be one fold and one shepherd" and "that they all may be one." They have all accepted as a commission meant for them a command to go into all the world and baptize in the name of the one Father and of the one Lord and of the one Spirit. When they recall the words recorded as spoken by the Lord on the night that he was betrayed—"Take, eat; this is my body"—all of the major divided communities of Christians take the words as meant for them and for all who are Christians. These are shared memories of all the separated church families, and all of them view their own life as continuous with the life out of which those memories come.

Furthermore, they all read, as descriptions of the common life into which they have entered and into which they summon others to enter, familiar apostolic testimonies: "So we, being many, are one body in Christ, and every one members of one another"; "We being many are one bread and one body"; "There is neither Jew nor Greek, there is neither bond nor free, there is neither male nor female; for ye are all one in Christ Jesus"; "There is one body and one Spirit . . . one Lord, one faith, one baptism, one God and

Father of all, who is above all and through all and in you all."

What and where is the Church to which these words refer? Is it an utterly invisible community unrelated to all the actual bodies which claim the name? Is it some one among the many?

We cannot meet the churches without coming to know the Church, and however we approach the Church we are compelled to recognize the oneness that belongs to it. All the great symbols and images used in Scripture to represent the Church are symbols of unity, of many bound together—flock, family, body, temple, household, a people. Nor need we look far to discover the deepest ground for the unity which marks the Church in both its nature and its calling. As the late Archbishop Temple said at Edinburgh in 1937, "The unity of the Church . . . is grounded in the unity of God and the uniqueness of his redeeming act in Jesus Christ. The 'one body and the one Spirit' correspond to the 'one God and Father of all.'" Alike in the Old Testament and in the New, there is the constant testimony to the one people who are in their communal existence both the answer to and the instrument of the one God.

Just what the oneness is which belongs to the Church, we shall find it hard to say. Let anyone who thinks it simple, try to unfold his meaning. Must the Church tolerate no diversity of thought or expression or ways? Must it speak everywhere one identical language? Must it be governed everywhere in one manner or submit everywhere to one this-world sovereignty? At least we know what is most clearly a scandal and a rock of offense among those who are called Christians: it is a lack of charity. For charity is acknowledged by all to be the most signal fruit of the one Spirit who dwells in the common life of those who have answered to Christ.

Whatever else it is, the Church is the community of those who gather in penitent wonder before the holy love of God coming to us in Christ, who worship that holy love in praise and thankfulness, and know themselves called to manifest it in their life together. "This is my commandment, that ye love one another as I have loved you." To be in charity with others is a deep kind of unity,

of at-one-ness. It is compatible with differences of opinion, even
with mutual criticism, though it labors in the face of these as does
profound family affection. But for those who are called Christ's
people to be at enmity with one another, to withdraw from one
another, to have no intimate, brotherly dealing with one another,
is a scandal. It is a scandal even to the unbelieving and half-
believing world around us.

It is a scandal when those who claim to be of one parentage,
given birth and nurture in one sacrificial love, do not speak or visit
in one another's houses, do not break bread together at high family
festivals, do not pray for one another or with one another. For
again, whatever else it is, the Church is the family and household
of God, the company of those who have received the Spirit by
which they can cry together, "Abba, Father," "Our Father." When
in a natural family we learn that one part no longer speaks to
another part, that there are no friendly visits back and forth between houses, that they do not come together for the breaking of
bread, that one even rejoices when it gets ahead at the expense of
the other— we judge that something is very wrong. Is it otherwise
with the family of God?

It is a strange spectacle when those who call the world in
recognizably common terms to be reconciled are themselves un-
reconciled. To quote Archbishop Temple again: "We call the
world . . . that its divisions may be healed and that it may find
fellowship in Him . . . And the world answers, 'Have you found
that fellowship yourselves? Why do your voices sound so various?
When you pass from words to action, to what are you calling us?
Is it to one family gathered round the holy table, where your Lord
is himself the host who welcomes all his guests? You know that
it is not so. When we answer your united call, we have to choose
for ourselves to which table we will go, for you are yourselves
divided in your act of deepest fellowship and by your own traditions
hinder us from a unity we are ready to enjoy.' "[1]

---

[1] *Faith and Order* (Edinburgh Conference Report), edited by Leonard
Hodgson (New York: The Macmillan Co., 1938), p. 18.

We call the world, burdened with its own tragic divisions of race and class and nationality, to find its unity in the one Father and the one Christ, and then we add other divisions to those with which it already struggles. "Woe unto the world because of offenses." The simple are confused and the sensitive are offended by the incongruity between the churches and the Church.

A supply pastor was calling on an isolated family in a little New England township. He had prayers with the family and noticed that the children in saying the Lord's Prayer used the words, "Forgive us our trespasses." He asked the older boy whether they were Episcopalians. The boy replied, "I don't know what we are, but we ain't what Reverend X is" (naming the pastor of the one church in the township). All the boy knew was that the only actual embodiment of the Church within reach was not *his*.

During the war, it was not unusual for a Roman Catholic soldier or sailor to stray into an Episcopal celebration of the Holy Communion. There were outward likenesses with the sacrament familiar to him, and differences too. Sometimes he received the sacrament and then asked with some perplexity whether this had been a "Catholic" service. Perhaps it was for him a time of crisis before battle; what was he to be told? Had he entered into communion with Christ, or hadn't he? Had the Church ministered unto him, or hadn't it?

A clergyman of a particular denomination is serving as "Protestant chaplain" in a large mental hospital; he is appointed and supported by the local federation of churches. The hospital authorities cannot deal with a multitude of churches. The chaplain believes that the Lord's Supper or Communion is specially needed by these sick spirits. The patients are of many churches; they want what is familiar and recognizably their own. They want to be assured that this is their own church coming to them, their own ministry and their own communion. What can he offer them that is not divisive?

In a Japanese internment camp there was a large group of a particular church family. They greatly desired the comfort of the

Lord's Supper in their loneliness and dread, but there was no ordained minister of their own kind among them. Finally some of them asked an ordained minister from another church family to give them the Lord's Supper according to the form in which they had been nurtured. He gladly consented. But this divided the group of the very church family it was meant to serve: some of them had been taught that they should seek communion with their Lord only at the hands of one who bore the authority of their own particular church.

In Australia, a missionary conference is held representing nearly all the non-Roman communions working in the south Pacific area. For the most part these bodies work in clearly defined areas, and there is little overlapping. But native Christians do not remain tidily in one missionary area. When they move into the area assigned to another church, do they have the privilege of fellowship and find a church which is unquestionably their own? How can they, if there are barriers to intercommunion and no ministries recognized by all? Those who meet to plan together for the practical concerns of the Church's mission are constantly driven to wrestle with the problem of the many churches.

Because there is something false and incoherent in the relation between the many churches and the one Church, it does not work. We turn to the churches, and they bear witness to the one Church. We look for the Church, and find the churches. Where is the Church among the churches?

To that disturbing question there are a number of answers which are possible and are actually given. The tidiest answer is given by Roman Catholicism; it is the view that among all the bodies popularly known as churches, there is and can be but one that is in very truth *the* Church. This one has clear, visible marks and boundaries. It has its center of this-world allegiance in the vicar of Christ in Rome. None of the other bodies, it says, are truly of the Church, though they may have elements of faith and practice which go into the making of the Church and could be taken up into it if the faithful returned in obedience to their rightful allegiance.

According to another view, there are among the many so-called churches certain bodies which possess the unmistakable marks that qualify them as truly of the Church. Other bodies do not qualify. The few true churches taken together are the Church, or are branches of the Church even though divided and not in communion with one another. The remaining groups are variously called "denominations" or "sects" or "Christian bodies." They may manifest many admirable Christian traits or gifts, but they are not churches in the true sense of the word. This view is held by some Episcopalians or Anglicans. It is sometimes called the "three-branch theory," since in its chief form it recognizes the Roman Catholic Church, the Orthodox churches, and the Anglican churches as the three branches of the true Church.

Widespread in Protestantism is the conviction that there are certain recognizable marks of the Church which are present in many degrees of fullness or dilution in practically all the churches. These marks are the profession of the faith given to men by God in the Scriptures and the carrying on of the ancient sacraments or ordinances of baptism and the Lord's Supper. Where these are, there is the Church, whether or no those who adhere to them are bound together in visible community. And this view may be watered down to mean little more than that whatever calls itself a church presumably is a church. The Church is then simply the sum total of all the churches.

Finally, we must recognize that the thought has had wide currency that in the deepest sense the Church is a hidden reality, known only to God. It is a secret society whose members cannot even know one another with assurance, the secret society of the truly faithful, truly elect, truly converted. It is not to be identified with the churches at all, though its members may be found within any or all of them or quite outside of them.

Plainly, men differ as to how they conceive of the Church and how they identify it. We must clarify these differences if we are even to understand our problem, let alone find clues for its solution.

CHAPTER II

The Will for Unity

Facing the stubbornly divided churches we would be as men without hope if there were not, moving through the churches, a will for unity. We must not exaggerate romantically the drive or diffusion of that will; no man can measure these imponderables accurately. The will for unity, or the dream of a united Church, is seemingly very faint in many parts of the total Christian community. But looking into the years behind us and looking out onto the churches as we see them, we can discern this will working.

As we look back over the long history of the Christian movement, we can see that it has always been marked by a struggle for unity in the face of powerful forces constantly threatening or actually creating division. There is no reason to suppose it will ever be otherwise on this earth. Any unity we achieve among men will be hard to win and hard to keep.

Already in the first century, St. Paul was struggling to maintain unity in the face of divisive forces within and among the local communities which were the spiritual offspring of his apostleship. Their unity was threatened by divisive groupings around popular leaders, by the self-absorption of the local community forgetful of its responsible part in the wider fellowship, by the pride of those who adhered rigorously to the old letter and the pride of those who were sure that they were moved by the new Spirit. At the end of the first century, the moving words of the Fourth Gospel reflect the consciousness that the Lord of the Church ever pleads that his friends shall be one even as he and the Father are one.

The summons out of the primitive witness has never ceased to echo in the ears of Christian people, but the emphasis and application it received have varied greatly through the centuries. We look back on what is often called the period of the undivided Church, roughly the first thousand years. Even the amateur church historian knows that the church of that period can be called "undivided" only by a refusal to count as church in any significant sense any of the streams which broke away from the main stream. Yet a substantial, dominant unity was maintained until the great division between the catholicism of the East and the catholicism of the West. But it was a hard-won unity—some would say, maintained at too great a cost to other precious values.

The familiar divisive forces, in all their complicated interplay, were constantly working. Honest differences over the true interpretation and formulation of the faith; differences regarding observances and worship, differences regarding church discipline; the rivalries of ambitious leaders, power politics, local loyalties, cultural and sociological diversities—were pulling the Christian community apart. In that period we see the church wrestling to maintain its unity, and fashioning some of its most characteristic organs for that very purpose among others: creating one canon of Holy Scripture, formulating its historic creeds, developing its bishops as symbols and instruments of unity in the great centers and its councils of bishops as organs of common counsel, finally in the West developing its papacy as the uniting sovereign authority. We cannot evade the sorry comment that some of these instrumentalities, brought into being to guard the church's unity, came later to be grounds for division.

After the great schism between East and West, the church of the West maintained an impressive though not untroubled unity until the Reformation. At the very least, we can say that for ancient and medieval catholicism and for the great reformers the Church's visible unity was unquestionably viewed as normal, belonging to the Church's nature, and division was seen as abnormal, a condition of sickness, something to be recovered from. And to the credit of catholicism in all its major expressions, it should be said that it has never lost hold of the notes of unity and universality, even though the very character of the unity it has sought to maintain or impose has been a ground for rebellion among free and creative spirits.

While the reformers truly sought to find unity among themselves, the forces of division they helped to set free were too strong for them and their successors. The mind and spirit of Luther left their characteristic marks on the conservatively reformed churches that emerged in Germany and Scandinavia. The mind and spirit of Calvin were strongly impressed on the more radically reformed churches of France, Switzerland, Holland and Scotland. The church in England was reshaped less drastically as reforming zeal was held in check by royal caution. With revolution on the march, ecclesiastically left-wing Anabaptists and other enthusiastic sects grew in strength to frighten conservative reformers hardly less than they frightened the Catholic hierarchy or the Catholic princes.

In the centuries that followed, the process of fragmentation went further as the passion for a pure and biblical church swept past the dikes within which the governments and conservative reformers had sought to hold it. Congregationalists and Baptists were the result. And so it went on through the eighteenth century and into the early nineteenth. The contagious and disciplined piety of Methodism broke with the Church of England, weary of passion and complacent with political privilege and eighteenth-century reasonableness. Unitarianism and Universalism broke with Calvinistic Congregationalism in the interests of that same eighteenth-century reasonableness and of a higher estimate of man's capacities. Lutheranism was divided on national lines. Presbyterianism and the Baptist churches were subdivided commonly by the divergent interpretations of the very Scriptures which were supposed to guarantee unity. And then the glacial movements of migration from Europe to the New World deposited all this in a chaotic pattern upon the great spaces of this country, where ecclesiastical "free enterprise" has had such an opportunity as nowhere else on the earth.

We need not elaborate on our own American contribution to the process of fragmentation: the divisions of major Protestant church families between north and south, the emergence of the great Negro denominations with Baptist and Methodist associations, strong communions such as the Disciples issuing from an honest effort to find a primitive biblical basis for the overcoming of disunity. Nor need we explore the fringe, where a friend of mine discovered somewhere in the southwest a "Separated Church of Unity."

In retrospect, it appears that the tide which had been running so long toward division, turned about one hundred years ago. Nothing is more mysterious in our human history than the great turnings of the tide in man's striving. We explain them in terms of reaction: men have had enough of one group of values, and seek complementary or even antithetical values; enough of order, and want freedom; enough of convention, and want spontaneity; enough of freedom, and there is a flight from freedom. We refer the great turnings of history to the mystery of leadership and to the mystery of providence, but in the end we are left facing the sheer givenness of the fact.

If I may illustrate the change in climate in terms of the history of my own church, the preface to our first American Prayer Book of 1789 refers to "the different religious denominations of Christians in these States," and to the fact that as a result of the independence of the American states these denominations "were left at full and equal liberty to model and organize their respective Churches, and forms of worship, and discipline, in such manner as they might judge most convenient for their future prosperity." The "different religious denominations of Christians" were accepted without question and apparently without any searching of heart, as was their continuance into the future. Now, one hundred and fifty years later, the Prayer Book contains a prayer that we may "seriously lay to heart the great dangers we are in by our unhappy divisions," and this church is deeply involved on many fronts in a struggle for unity which seriously disturbs its own inner life, yet from which it cannot and would not disengage itself.

The influences and motives which flowed together to feed the reviving will to unity at work within the churches are too numerous for any complete analysis. Some of the influences are quite secular, of the world, such as new possibilities for travel and communication and the constant movement of populations. All the factors which have been carrying us with frightening speed to one world have played their part and will continue to. The world in which most men and women lived most of their lives in one region with fairly settled neighbors was favorable to settled and exclusive loyalties. We and the generation just before us have lived in a world in which the interpenetration of all our inherited human groupings of every sort has been constantly accelerated. Presbyterians, Methodists, Baptists, Lutherans, Episcopalians, Roman Catholics live side by side, work together, play together, go to school together, marry one another. Barriers must be strong to withstand that steady pressure of association. Men are faced increasingly with alternatives of antagonisms heightened by close contact or of tolerance that can lead to mutual appreciation and the discovery of deep kinship. Borrowing is easy—borrowing of hymns, of books learned and unlearned, of architecture, of preachers.

It is not strange that in such a world individuals faced with the same problems, moved by the same concerns, and discovering that they have such a large measure of common inheritance, began to associate themselves together for Christian purposes quite apart from church divisions. The Young Men's Christian Association and the Young Women's Christian Association, founded in the middle years of the last century, are familiar examples of Christians from many church backgrounds united for a Christian work. Bible societies and certain missionary societies with interdenominational membership and the Student Christian Movement come to mind as further examples.

Such associations and cooperative activities of Christian individuals do not directly affect the separation of the churches out of which those individuals come. This is not to minimize in the least the service these agencies contribute to the common Christian cause. Nor is it to minimize the indirect influence they have had in establishing personal contact between the membership and the leadership of the churches. The Student Christian Movement has nurtured in England and in Europe some of the finest leadership of the church unity movement. Men and women whose missions have taken them back and forth between the divided denominations could not rest content with the isolationism of their own or other churches. So while Christian unity in this sense is no solution for the frustrations and incongruities of the divided churches, it does provide a soil in which the will for unity can be nurtured.

The inner motives which are the substances of this will struggling for fulfillment within the divided churches can be divided into three interwoven strands.

The motive which is probably most immediately intelligible to practical-minded Americans is the concern for economy or efficiency in the performance of the church's work. This includes not only the strictly economic interest in the saving of money and materials, but the higher economy of manpower and of spiritual resources, the shaping of the instruments for the most effective and least wasteful performance of the task.

In thousands of small American communities, little half-starved churches of various denominations, with underpaid ministers and utterly inadequate facilities, have struggled for existence. It is no wonder that in many hundreds of such communities people have turned to the desperate remedy of the "community church"—desperate because it is a purely local solution and brings into being isolated congregations, without wide relationships or oversight, which must draw their ministries from more settled churches. And these detached local congregations, seeking to remedy their lack, tend to reach out in search of association, to form still another denomination. Whole areas of rural America are settling back into virtual godlessness, thanks to the impotence of a divided church to bring Christian teaching and pastoral oversight and fellowship and prayer to scattered families. Our whole approach to the Christian nurture of the coming generation is literally hamstrung by our divisions, and we are driven back on the baffling feebleness of our Sunday schools. In many a great hospital, hundreds of suffering and lonely men and women are very inadequately ministered to by the churches, because we cannot all go in, and who will go for us?

The assumption underlying this motive for unity is that the many bodies concerned are doing or are capable of doing substantially the same work; that as teaching bodies they are teaching substantially the same things; that as communities of witness they are proclaiming essentially the same gospel; that they offer men effectual means of spiritual help and ways of communion with the same God. If that assumption is not accepted, implicitly or explicitly, all considerations of economy break down. It is just the churches with the strongest conviction of having something distinctive or indispensable to bring to men that are least moved by these practical considerations.

The second and more deep-going motive is that which arises from the very nature of Christian faith and of the Church. A religion which proclaims the brotherhood of men in God's family, which links love for men with love for God, which views the Church as the household of God, the body of Christ and the this-world sacrament of the Kingdom which is to come, cannot be content with a radically divided Church. "The call to unity is primarily from God to man," as Bishop Brent said in the opening sermon at the Lausanne Conference on Faith and Order. "It is God who takes the lead; His will that they all be one must eventually be man's will, if to do God's will becomes the passion of the human heart. When Christians accept Christ as supreme, they cannot but walk as companions and friends."

I know only too well the answers that rise to quiet our consciences. Do you really expect all the divisions and multiplicity that are in man—yes, all the riches that God has granted us in our divisions—to be brought into any recognizable unity? Is not what you are speaking of for heaven rather than for earth? Do you or does God want a drab uniformity of Christian witness and worship? Is there not a healthy diversity among us?

To which the answers might be: Humanly speaking, this *is* too much to expect. So is it too much to expect that we should become the wholehearted servants of the love of God, but we stand under judgment while it remains unattained. It *is* a thing of heaven, but are we not taught to pray, "Thy will be done on earth as it is in heaven"? Neither God nor man wants a drab uniformity. God is richness and the eternal source of variety; we are creatures and finite, able to see and appreciate only fragments of his truth and beauty. But in our divisions we hold his manifold gifts apart from one another in proud and mutually impoverishing separation.

That is the third strand in the will for unity—the need for wholeness, our impoverishment without the enrichment of one another's gifts. We Episcopalians believe in offering man the sacrament of our Lord's death for us and of our Lord's victory for us, in shining chalice with fair linen; we might learn from Presbyterians not to offer men the Word of God in shabby and ill-prepared speech. We are seldom silent in church; we might learn from the Friends the power of a silent reaching down of the human spirit into the still working of the Holy Spirit. Each of us according to his own inheritance can add to the catalogue of the precious things we could receive from others from whom we are now divided.

The will to unity is alive and struggling within the churches. Within all the varieties of human motives, faith can discern the hand of God. As always, he has guided us by the stern "must" of outer circumstances and by the inspired wisdom of prophetic leaders. By the necessities of impoverished congregations, by the harsh disclosure of the feebleness and scandal of our competitive and divided witness, by the scorn of men for unintelligible differences, by the prophetic judgment that "the world is too strong for a divided church," God has shaken many of us out of our complacent acceptance of disunity and led us to where we stand. He has driven us together and called us together. Anyone who has had a part in this struggle of the churches to be the Church is often asked, "Have you got anywhere with this business?" To which the answer surely is that God has taken us far, considering that he has *us* to work with, but he will not let us rest here.

The progress made even in the past few decades is something to wonder at and to rejoice in, in a world where there is so much darkness and enmity. With the major exception of Roman Catholicism, it has affected greatly the life and relationships of all the great church families and most of their subdivisions. Cooperation and agencies of cooperation have grown steadily. Home and foreign missionary boards and educational departments of many churches regularly take counsel together and have created ably staffed organs for dealing with their shared problems. The Federal Council of Churches in the United States and similar organizations in other lands have won the wholehearted adherence of churches that at first held back. In our larger cities, local federations provide means by which most of the major non-Roman churches can work together for the sick and imprisoned, for a more intelligent and less crassly competitive placement of new churches in developing areas, for common action in dealing with social ills and in relations with public authorities.

On a world scale, the developing World Council of Churches kept open the communications between churches in enemy lands throughout the Second World War. It initiated the quick meeting of church leaders when open warfare ended. It has provided a channel through which aid could flow from the church people of America and England and Sweden to the churches in hungry and blasted Europe and Asia. And the World Council holds out the hope of an established agency of common counsel for the leadership of the many member churches. Its very existence serves to deepen our realization that beneath all our divisions we Christian people have a common cause and calling.

Side by side with this impressive growth in cooperative relations has come substantial progress in the strengthening of ties and in corporate union within and across the lines of church families. The territorial groupings of Lutheranism and also of Anglicanism, for

example, have far closer relationships within their own communions than was the case fifty years ago. In these and in other
great church families there has been a growing consciousness of the
Church as a world fellowship. That is something to be gratefully
welcomed, even though the strengthening of confessional ties on
a world scale may complicate progress towards unity across denominational lines. Divisions of Presbyterianism have been healed in
Scotland, and of Methodism in this country. In Canada a great
United Church, including Methodist, Congregational and Presbyterian elements, has celebrated its twenty-second birthday.

After years of prayer and conference, there has come into existence a United Church of South India, which has taken up into its
life Methodists, Episcopalians, Presbyterians and Congregationalists. Conversations are going on in Australia, in Canada and in
the United States involving non-Episcopal and Episcopal churches.
Even when they stumble and pause, these conversations educate
and stir consciences and define issues.

A process of searching and mutually respectful conferences on
a worldwide scale has taken root and is being carried on by the
conferring scholars of many traditions, inclusive of Eastern Catholicism, Anglo-catholicism, churches of the classical Protestant tradition, and churches of the freer Protestant type. The many churches
sharing in this process are being driven to ask themselves and to
ask one another what they mean by "church" and "word" and
"sacrament" and "ministry." They are discovering that they often
mean quite different things by the same word and often use
different words to mean the same thing.

It would be very false to deny that our goal, however defined,
certainly if defined as a truly united Church, is very far off. To
those of us who stand outside Roman Catholicism, it appears that
that great church remains immovable—stiffening, it would seem,
and becoming less approachable. Yet prayers are said for us there.
To be sure, they are chiefly prayers for our "return," but among
the finest spirits in that ancient household these are not all
complacent prayers; they are not wholly without the note of self-

criticism. Would it not be well if prayers were said among us for them? For surely it is for just those who are furthest from us, for those hardest for us to understand, for those who are ecclesiastically our "enemies," that we are specially bidden to pray. And our prayers could well include thanksgiving that so many of God's children have there been brought to their knees and found assurance of forgiveness and strength to meet life's sorrows.

This need not exclude the solemn conviction that there are proud pretensions there which we cannot accept, even dangerous errors. But are there no proud pretensions among us and have no errors crept in? Unquestionably the widest chasm in the Christian community is the Catholic-Protestant chasm, but we cannot simply accept it as something irrevocably given, for plainly Christ is finding men and being found of men on both sides of that chasm. Where Christ is, there in some elemental sense is the Church, and the will for unity must reach out.

Cooperative federation in the forms widely achieved among the non-Roman communions, though it has high values, direct and indirect, does not satisfy the will to unity. It leaves us reproducing our divisions and it does not reach down into the central sanctities of the churches' lives, to the level of faith and shared utterance, to the level of common prayer and communion and pastoral relationship. One is not baptized into a federation. A federation does not provide the all-one-body experience. It does not knit together in one communion and fellowship. It does not nurture its membership in a shared faith. It has no sacraments or ordinances. To be the ministerial representative of a federation is at best a makeshift. A federation is not a church; it is a league of churches non-communicating, unashamedly competitive churches; but it is far from satisfying the meaning of "one body in Christ."

Intercommunion, as widely practiced among Protestant churches, is not in itself the answer to our striving. It commonly means an unquestioning extension of guest privileges among communions at one another's "holy tables." The refusal of such privileges is a greater offense than the granting of them is a strong cement. Some might be tempted to say that communion is most "open" where "holy table" and "altar" have come to have a less meaningful part in the life of the churches. That would, I believe, be too harsh a judgment. But in any case the sharing in the ordinance of the Lord's Supper or the sacrament of Holy Communion is not to be treated as a thing apart. It has little power or meaning save as it is the sacramental accompaniment of a shared faith and a responsible, committed life in community. Rigorous conditions of admission to communion may be the expression of proud and overexclusive pretensions, but they may also reflect the conviction that this is a responsible relationship. One cannot simply "walk in" on it without commitment to the life of which this is a most holy expression. For two divided churches to declare that they are "in communion" with one another, and then to go their own ways without taking counsel, without sharing burdens, without binding responsibilities, without any heavy commitments, is, to say the least, a not very costing form of unity.

The unions of previously separated churches which have been achieved are heartening. They help us to believe that the forces of healing are overcoming the forces of disintegration. Yet one must honestly say that these unions are not yet of an extent to change radically the over-all picture of the divided Church. And as things are, and as things so commonly are in our world, the solutions reached bring with them new problems. The United Church of Canada is a happy solution for Canada but by that very fact it is another "kind" among churches, no longer part of world Methodism or world Presbyterianism. We must pray that the United Church of South India will prove a blessing in South India, but there are those who ask anxiously, "What is the relation now of the former Anglicans who have entered that union, to the Anglican communion?" To which the answer is as yet not very clear.

The God-given will for unity will ever struggle for a situation in which the "Church" as something actualized, not simply as something hidden, is in the foreground, and the diversities of gifts and apprehensions represented by "the churches" are gathered into it in mutually enriching interplay.

The obstacles in the way are legion and are of many orders. Certainly they are not all in the realm of what we call "faith" or of what we call "order" buttressed by faith. That most versatile human vice of pride is a major obstacle: group pride; pride that we have bishops or that we haven't; pride that we have a liturgy or that we haven't; pride in being different from some other human group. Pride and littleness and lethargy, these stand in the way, and sentimental clinging to the familiar even by those who have ceased to make use of it. Vested interests stand in the way. There are always those who would rather be big fish in a little puddle than little fish in a big puddle. Very widely in America a chief obstacle is a small local view of the Church that has no image of its majesty and universal meaning. Along with these ugly things, and sometimes hard to distinguish from them, stands tenacious loyalty to that which has brought precious values into one's life, and a rightful refusal to take any step which would repudiate or dishonor a good inheritance.

Strong as are the non-theological obstacles, there is no escaping the fact that deep differences of faith and of underlying assumptions stand in the way, too. Around these real differences all the other forces in the way gather and intrench themselves.

The will for unity is at work among us. Our task must be to waken and feed the aspiration where it is dormant or feeble. No will can grow that can see no direction to move in and is held back by unanalyzed, almost unconscious fears and inhibitions. We must seek to clarify the goals of the will for unity, to prospect imaginatively for paths in which it can move, so that it does not die of despair and frustration. We must pull up out of our corporate memories the confused and half-buried prejudices and fears and misunderstandings that hold us back from full and free communion with our fellows. It may be said devoutly that only God can give us such a will and bring it to good effect. But surely our human part is to prepare the way of the Lord and to do all within our power to make his paths straight.

CHAPTER III

The Church as Body and Spirit

We meet with the churches, in the plural, and find them speaking of the Church, in the singular. We find those who are divided affirming the unity of that which they profess to be, its unity in reality or in hope and intention. To borrow some illuminating phrases from Richard Niebuhr and turn them to our present purpose, when a church asks, "What must I become in order that I may be myself?" a part of the answer is, "I ought to be one, one in Christ." When we ask, "What is or what should be the unity which makes the Church?" every divided communion shows a very natural disposition to reply, "It is such unity as you find among *us.*"

The Roman Catholic protests earnestly that we must all find our unity within that great institution, in faithful allegiance to the sovereign vicar of Christ in Rome. The Anglican dreams of a commonwealth of territorial churches, of episcopal churches in communion with one another, holding together the faith embodied in the creeds of ancient catholicism, sharing the great sacraments, taking regular counsel together for their worldwide concern. The Lutheran bids us not be too much concerned with structure and organization, but to find our unity in a shared faith, particularly that apprehension of the faith found in the great Lutheran formularies. The Baptist urges us to beware of all centralization of "human" authority and the tyranny of "human" forms, and to seek a free association of independent congregations faithful to God's truth and God's ordinances.

A chief part of our task must be to try to uncover the roots of these differences among the many churches about the one Church. If we ask each of the divided churches to speak for itself, we shall find that each will speak in its own favorite terms from within its own intrenched position. We must try to draw one another out into more neutral territory, where if possible our settled differences can be undercut and we can break through the patterns of thought with which we confront one another. Neutral ground will be best provided by areas of shared experience in which we can all feel at home. Two such areas are our life in a family and our life as members of "a people." These are two analogies to "church" used in the Bible more than any others. The Church is a family, a realm of sonship and brotherhood; the Church is the "people of God." Let us develop these analogies and seek clues in them for our problem.

There is one fact about the many churches which can be expressed in many ways. This is the fact that they include in their existence what I shall call a bodily or external or visible aspect, and a spiritual or inner or invisible aspect. It could not be otherwise, since churches consist of human persons in relations with one another and with One whom they call God.

Human persons are embodied spirits. They have an inner life which we indicate variously by speaking of their thoughts, beliefs, feelings, affections, wills. But this interior or spiritual life is met with, either in ourselves or in others, only in connection with the visible, tangible, outer fact we call bodies. Our minds and hearts make contact with others through the medium of our bodies and their bodies, or through that common, visible, audible, tangible world of which our bodies are part. To have fellowship with another or with a group of others always involves the bodily or outward or sensory, directly or indirectly.

Society or social experience is a possibility whenever or wherever two or three meet. And by meeting we normally mean coming into another's bodily presence, within sight of his body, especially of his face, within the sound of his voice, within the reach of his hand. To meet another is normally to look at him, to say something and to reach out and touch. Then inner things begin to happen. We communicate, most explicitly by language but also by signs or expressions, intended or unconscious. The outward which makes possible our meeting is not confined to the bodily, but includes the common world of sense, the place where we meet, what we do together, the other bodily presences. We may call in a wider world of potentially shared experiences, memories of places where we have both been or of other embodied spirits we have both met.

I sit beside a stranger in a train. There is another human body next to my body. I assume that where there is a human body there is a human mind, where a human exterior, a human interior. I take sidelong glances at his clothes, his hands, what he reads, his face, seeking for clues as to what manner of man this is. Our eyes meet and we smile. I say, "Nice day, isn't it?" seeking common ground and knowing there is nothing more common than the weather. Perhaps I say, "Where are you from?" and then taking a long shot go on, "Do you know So-and-so?" We seek common ground in a common world of outer fact and inner meaning, and finding it we say we have really met.

Of course we must say of these casual, fragmentary forms of human meeting that while the actual bodily presence and the common world, shared directly or indirectly, are indispensable means and offer the possibility, yet they do not of themselves guarantee a meeting, let alone fellowship. For that, the unseen and spiritual are necessary. I may go to meet another and find him asleep, or withdrawn, as we say, or so hostile that "we could find nothing in common." It could be that in the body next to me the mind is all gone.

Our deeper and more settled forms of relationship involve these same elements in more clearly defined ways. Marriage is surely recognized as one of the most intimate and significant forms of human association. We speak of a man and a woman as being "united" in marriage and of the relationship as a "union." But we also speak of them as being "made one flesh." Obviously the uniqueness of this relationship is found in what is at once bodily and affectional, of the spirit. We view these two elements as rightly joined together, the special form of love and the bodily relationship in which that special form of love is expressed, actualized and nurtured. And added to this central bodily core there is a vast amount of having outward things in common—a house, possessions, children—all of which are the continuing occasions for a rich and varied inward sharing of meanings, experiences, hopes, fears. There is normally added a legal bond, fortifying the relationship with the compulsions of wider social controls.

We commonly say that marriage is present where these outward and identifiable conditions are found—legal ties properly formulated and recorded, the bodily union, the continuing community in outer life. Yet the full quota of outer marks does not guarantee the inward reality of marriage, the hidden mutuality which is its animating spirit. If two persons so related outwardly, grow apart inwardly, the bodily and outward community may become intolerable. We strive, with imperfect success, to be assured that the spirit is present before the union is formalized. We seek to be assured of inward consent. On the other hand, society has been compelled to recognize that this spiritual reality may actualize itself without due legal form, and we could hardly deny the name of marriage to some relationships which are deprived, by sickness or other circumstances, of aspects of bodily community normally constitutive of marriage.

Out of marriage commonly come children and a family. To be someone's child is certainly a bodily relationship, and likewise to be someone's brother. It is noteworthy that ordinarily we use the term "a relation" or "a relative" to mean a person to whom we are linked "by blood" or "by marriage." We expect parents to begin treating their child as "theirs" as soon as he is born, long before he is capable of spiritual response, let alone has shown any evidences of moral worth. Usually they do; they do not wait to discover whether he is spiritually congenial or responsive.

None of us deny the bodily aspect in that form of human association we call the family. We recognize that over and above its basis in biological relatedness, a family requires for its well-being, if not for its very being, a common house, a common table, and many occasions for face-to-face meeting. Most people find it difficult to look upon an illegitimate child with the same eyes with which they see a legitimate one. But equally we know that a family is not constituted simply by the bodily or biological facts or by legal facts. It is a thing of the spirit—family spirit—of parental love, filial love and brotherly love. Where these are almost entirely absent we are inclined to say, "That is no real family." It has failed too utterly to actualize the "ought" within its own being.

I read recently of twin brothers returning from war service, who met for the first time their "own" sister. Their mother having died soon after their birth, they had been adopted by another family, and grew to manhood without knowing their "real" father or their sister. So closely do we adhere to the bodily in our thoughts and feelings about family that we refer to their father-after-the-flesh as their "real" father and to their blood-sister as their "own" sister. Yet it could well be that these young men were so thoroughly adopted into their foster family, so fully taken up into the outer and inner aspects of its life, that their deep-going relationships were all with the adopting family. To which family do they belong? Bodily relationship, legal relationship, spiritual relationship normally belong together, but they may become separated. It is not wholly uncommon for some person to be taken into a family that has no blood or legal relationship with him. We say, "He is really one of the family." But there would be no family to be "one of" without the bodily base and the wider base of outwardly and inwardly shared life.

Furthermore, family relationship is not limited to those who are tied together in marriage or are the common offspring of a particular couple, and who have lived together under one roof or broken bread at a common table. It reaches out to include the seldom seen and the unseen. It includes an aunt living in a distant place or a grandfather who died years ago. By blood they are related to us, whether we realize it or not. But we may come to realize this relationship and have a strong consciousness of community with them without ever meeting them; without meeting them, but not without the participation of the outward and the inward.

The unseen "relations" with whom I have the most lively sense of connection are those whose pictures, whose letters, tales of whose doings have been shared with me by those related to them and to me. I have made a pilgrimage to the old house of a grandfather whom I never knew in the flesh, though I have made my own my parents' memory of my being taken there in infancy. In some cases, things that were once the possessions of unseen relations are now mine—an old chair, a bureau, a mirror, a letter. A family cannot maintain a strong and widespreading sense of relatedness save as it treasures the outward things and images and verbalized memories and documents which are part of its common life.

The family is the outstanding example of that form of human society which is marked by intimate, face-to-face relationships, the constant renewal of bodily nearness and therefore the possibility of much conversation and intercommunication by bodily signs. Just for these reasons, the family is markedly informal, spontaneous, free in its relations. At its best, it lives largely by the law of love and requires little appeal to law or to the more impersonal claims of justice. Yet it is greatly guarded and given structure and stability by legal forms and by the "quiet tyranny of custom." Because of this character, the family serves as a standard for other intimate, close-knit fellowships. So we may speak of a small school community as having a family spirit.

By contrast, a "people" or a nation is an outstanding example of a multitude of ongoing lives knit together across wide spaces and over centuries. The multitude of individual lives and groups of lives—family groups, local communities, interest groups—which make up a people obviously do not meet, face to face, more than samplings of one another. What holds them together and makes them a people? It is not our task here even to approximate a full answer to that question. The chief point to be recognized is that here again we find the elements of body and spirit, the outward and the inward. Plainly, a people is in part a spiritual reality or, in more coldly scientific terms, an instance of social psychology. It is constituted by shared sentiments, thoughts, memories, hopes, loyalties, ideals, enmities, by a sense of community, by patriotism.

Simply to gather a million human beings into a given territory and fence them in would not be to constitute a people or a nation. That would be a vast concentration camp, a chaotic herd. But equally, the inner and spiritual elements that go to make a people do not arise and do not maintain themselves without the bodily and the exterior. Commonly, a people is knit together in part by a large measure of long continued intermarriage and intermingling of blood, so that it possesses a diffused sense of kinship, often supported by general bodily likeness, at least of color though not necessarily. Usually a people has long shared a land. Not all the people ever see all the land; they see their part of it and hear stories of other parts. But this land, these hills and cities and rivers and coasts, all belong to them together.

Normally a people shares a language. It treasures common memories of events and persons foundational for their common life. Memories are inward and spiritual, but these memories are not kept alive and certainly are not widely shared save as they take shape in shared verbal symbols and accounts and pictures and statues. The people of the United States share Washington and Lincoln, the Mayflower, Jamestown, Bunker Hill, through the verbal and pictorial images which are carried in their tradition. To diffused kinship, the homeland, the language, shared memories, we could add much else: little political creeds, such as "Government of the people, by the people, for the people"; words such as "democracy," with fluid meaning but charged with much sentiment; places and buildings meaningful for the common life, such as Lexington, Valley Forge, Plymouth Rock, the Supreme Court, the Capitol, the Lincoln Memorial; days we celebrate together; common folkways and institutions.

I suppose we could agree that all these things lie deeper than government or common law. A people is hardly ready for the constraints of government and a common law until it has come to know its members as in a large measure *one people*. Then it wants to go on in history together, and government and common law are essential for the ordering of any great human community. Once established, government becomes not only a necessary instrument of community but also a symbol of the people's life. Some at least of the highest offices and agencies of government become charged with meanings and potencies which outrun their practical services. When Americans rejoice that at a crisis in our history "the Union was preserved," they are moved not simply by practical or economic motives but by their sentiment for the total mystery of their common life as a people.

There are one or two other observations that are in order. One is that while a people clings to every major element which has found a central place in its historical life and serves as a bond for its present community and with its past, yet its existence as a community may survive the loss of precious and important bodily members. A people may be driven from its land and still survive as a people; it may be deprived of its government and survive as a people; it may have its capital and the great visible symbols of its continuing life destroyed and remain a people, conscious of its own continuing identity and recognizable to others. To use a biological analogy, the circulation and nerve channels essential for continuing life may find substitute routes, or a part of the body may take over the functions of other parts. A people may live with a marred and broken body, but it cannot live without *any* body, and it will not maintain its identity unless some of its body is carried through the tragedies and breaks of history to serve as a kind of root or transplanted "cutting" from which the outward life can be reconstituted.

Again, it must be observed in the case of a people as in that of a family that there is no absolutely fixed and guaranteed bond, no simple one-to-one correspondence between the body and the spirit of a people. The body may be found after the spirit of relationship

—"the spirit of 1776" or the founders—has begun to decay. Then the outer shape loses its vitality and meaning. Finally, broken fragments of the body in which the spirit once dwelt may be left lying about on the dumps of history or as museum pieces.

As in the case of the family, and surely to a greater degree, there are many who share outwardly in the life of a people who show little evidence of participating in its inner life. On the other hand, there are those who are not by birth or even by law citizens of a nation, who by participation in its life come to share deeply in the spirit of its people. Yet there would be no "American people" or "French people" if there were no "communal bodies" and no "bodies politic" holding the good, bad and indifferent members of these peoples in the bonds of a common life.

This may seem a long digression from our concern with the churches and the Church. As my readers may readily anticipate, my simple thesis is that Christian communities or churches show this same duality in their make-up as do these other familiar forms of human society of which I have been speaking. Furthermore, I believe that some of the most pervasive problems we face in the churches have to do with the relations of body and spirit in the being of the Church. If these ancient analogies of "the family" and "the people" are sound, they can be made to cut both ways with respect to some of the familiar contentions among the churches. On the one hand, they suggest that the bonds between particular outer forms or structures and the inner life are not as inflexible and exclusive as many would claim. On the other hand, they suggest that a church cannot be as careless of its body as many would have it be.

Viewed simply as forms of human association, the churches are obviously constituted by outer and inner aspects. The bodily aspects of churches are so manifold that it is difficult to take them in with completeness. In its most elemental, primitive form a church is marked by the assembling of persons in one another's bodily presence as a congregation, "two or three gathered together." The church is localized, made visible, in this assembly: there it is.

Normally the congregation builds a special house for its assembling. And as the building which houses the Supreme Court of the United States takes on the name and dignity of that which it houses, and is built in such a way as to express as well as to serve that purpose, so it is with the church's house. There are special words and forms of words which men use together when they assemble as church. Commonly there is a special man who is peculiarly the church's man, the minister. There are customary postures, which may be as simple as the contemplative posture of the Friends' meeting.

These are what we find in the simple local church of what is commonly called the Protestant type. To go where these things are found and used is to go to church, and to share in them is to share in church. The people meet by sharing in these things. Of course there are spiritual realities, without which the externals would collapse like a body out of which the life has gone, or be vacant like a body whose mind is gone. The people who meet together are bidden to come in faith and charity; they are summoned to praise, to contrition, to thankfulness; they are urged to pray inwardly, to repent inwardly, to rededicate themselves inwardly. We cannot see or hear or touch or measure faith and praise and interior prayer. We can say that John was in church today, or that fifty were there. But was John really there, inwardly there? He listened, or seemed to; he said the words; he bowed his head; he looked devout. But was he really listening? What did he hear? What did it mean to him? Did he mean what he said? Did he feel as he looked, or was he looking the way he thought people are supposed to look in church? And are there some who were not there in the body who *were* there in the spirit?

Church in its most elemental embodiment shows many similarities to the family. It is small, local. It can be relatively informal and spontaneous because it lives by often renewed, face-to-face meetings. It requires but few conventions, but little law. Granted that we do not find even here an infallible correspondence between body and spirit, we can judge with tolerable assurance who are really with us and of us. Yet, as in the family, we judge those to be with us and of us who share in the recognizable bonds of community. Church in its intimate, primitive form turns naturally to the language and symbols of the family life, as Jesus did. So church in that form can always find comfort and support in his words.

As we have already seen, church is found among us not only in little, informal, face-to-face groups, but also in far-spreading societies comparable to a people or a nation in their reach and membership. In the great churches, as in nations, we see multitudes of individuals and local groups of peoples held together in a common life without the possibility of personal acquaintance or the fellowship available to those who have personal acquaintance. In those great churches, what we are calling the bodily part is more formalized and elaborated, though not uniformly in the same ways. In general, they show a definite tendency to greater formalization of their outer life in terms of the verbalization of their faith, in ordinances and sacraments and other forms of worship, in ministries and laws and governments. It is surely not accidental that the great churches (using "great" as descriptive of their dimensions in space and time, without judgment of better or worse) are what we can call in general terms of the more "catholic" type. For a far-spreading society can maintain its character as a community only by achieving a body and connective tissue comparable to its reach. When the "little flock" of Jesus' days became a great community in fact or in hope, it quickly turned to the likeness of a people to express its own meaning.

We have been speaking thus of church as a form of human association marked by a horizontal relationship between men. But to do this is to omit just what is the most distinctive dimension in the nature of church. A church is certainly a form of human association, whether two or three are gathered together in face-to-face fellowship or a million are bound together in a single communion. But what distinguishes it as church is the fact that it views itself as in a kind of social relationship with God, with the Holy Other who is the primary object of religious concern. There is always a vertical reference in church; what goes on there and what is really constitutive is shared with God, however he may be conceived or symbolized. It is shared with the Father, with Christ, and with those who are with him, the saints. "Two or three gathered together," yes; but in his name or with him in the midst. Whatever God is not party to or does not have part in is not properly church.

Whatever we make of it, however we interpret it, however we view it as coming to pass, we can recognize this to be characteristic of churches as we find them in our contemporary world or in history. The place of worship is the home or temple of God's people in their character as his people. It is also his house, his temple. He owns it; he dwells there. "The Lord is in his holy temple." So his people gather there to meet with him. The book that is read there is the book of his people; the words spoken there are men's words, but the book and the words are likewise his or shared with him. The most distinctive actions, the sacraments or ordinances performed there, are acts of his people; they are also in some sense God's acts, or acts with reference to him. The minister or the priest is certainly a man, in a special sense the church's man, but he is likewise God's minister, God's priest. Even Christ, supremely Christ, as the central and originative meeting point of God and his people, partakes of this duality. He is God's Christ and man's Christ, God's and man's, God and Man.

In some cases the place, the words, the acts, the persons that serve as the meeting place, the means of communication or of communion between God and his people, are thought of as receiving this status or potency by the initiative of God. He appeared to Jacob at Bethel, so Jacob marked the place: he set up an altar there. This was a holy place. Jacob returned there to renew his meeting with God, and his descendants long held Bethel to be sacred.

Or, words took shape in the mind and on the lips of the prophet which he recognized as God's words to him and to God's people. These words embodied something of God's thought or judgment or will for his people. Through the medium of these words something in the mind of God was reaching out to the minds and hearts of men. The prophet uttered the words and some of God's people acknowledged them as from God. They treasured them and returned to them as men return to a holy place, to renew the meeting, to hear again God speaking.

Or, a man knew within himself that he had been laid hold of by God to speak to God's people in the name of God or to take them into God's presence. He communicated his conviction and began to play the part to which he knew himself called. Some of the people of God accepted him; they said among themselves, "God has given us this man to be our prophet, or our priest. When we seek to hear what God would say to us, or to come into his holy presence, let us turn to this man."

Or yet again, there was One who took bread and blessed it, and of whom it was said a little later that "he was made known to them in the breaking of bread." Men returned to this act as to a holy place, to renew their fellowship with him and in him with the Father.

On the other hand, some of the recognizable elements which the churches view as shared with God are thought of as receiving this status from the initiative of men. These things have been brought to God, dedicated, set apart, offered, consecrated, and God has accepted them and used them. The place has been built by us for him. The gifts have been offered by us to him, with the petition that he will take and bless them for his people. The words we speak or sing are our offering of prayer and praise to him. The man who ministers among us has been set apart by us to be peculiarly God's man.

These, then, are some of the basic stuff of which church is made—places, words, acts, persons, to which people turn together, or which they treasure together, for shared meeting with God. Some are viewed primarily as means or expressions of God's approach to his people; some are primarily means or expressions of his people's answer and approach to him. In either case they are held on to tenaciously because they have this meaning and potency, and they bind those who share in them into a distinctive form of community.

All these elements are "bodily" in the broad sense in which I am using that term. They are sensory in part; they can be seen or heard or touched. They are found in the world of space and time; we can know when and where they are present or absent. But, as has been inescapably implied in all our speaking of them, they all depend for their character and potency on spirit. The house is not "house of God" without the presence, and the presence is spirit. The word is not the word without meaning. The sacrament is not sacrament without communion or the possibility of communion. The uttered prayer is not prayer save as it is the bearer of prayer in the spirit.

So all these outer things collapse unless spirit is there—indwelling, animating, interpreting; God's Spirit and man's spirit. Or at the most they are left standing like dead things, still preserved by men out of aesthetic interest, antiquarian interest or scientific-historical interest.

Because these outward elements which are the bodily stuff of church are the common possession of God and man, they present a very special problem which appears and reappears in many forms. What men acknowledge to be God's or of God, takes on in their feeling and thought the qualities of God. It is holy, sacrosanct, charged with mystical power, perfect, untouchable, not given over to change and decay, immutable.

One need not look far to discover examples of this. The place where God has made himself known to men is a holy place. One must not touch anything there or change anything there. The temple, as God's dwelling place, is as abiding as God himself. It cannot be that he will permit it to be destroyed. The Bible, which is the word of God, is Holy Bible; it is the bearer of God's truth and therefore without error, not to be tampered with; nothing is to be taken away, nothing is to be added. The law which is God's is perfect law. The creed which declares the truth about God as he has revealed himself is for all times and for all places. The priests of God partake of his sanctity and of the sanctity of the holy things they handle. They must be without blemish. The ministers of God cannot be subject to the weaknesses of ordinary men. No profane or unclean thing must be uttered in their presence. The ordinances which are truly God's are forever and forever. Even the man who is truly God's can do no sin. "Whosoever is born of God doth not commit sin; . . . and he cannot sin because he is born of God" (I John 3:9).

Yet all these means by which God and man draw together are man's, too, and of man. Otherwise they could not serve as means of communication and communion. For even God and man can meet only by sharing, by having things in common, by finding a word which is a bearer of meaning for both, by coming to a meeting point. So the holy place is also a place in man's world, where Eli and his sons minister, perhaps. The temple is of stone that can be broken down. The Bible is man's word, too, and man's words stumble and slip and are relative to his passing times and his so partial knowledge. His thoughts are not as God's thoughts. The creeds which seek to catch the eternal in a net of words are always "dated." The priests are not without blemish, are even corrupted. The ministers are failing men. And the people of God are very imperfectly God's.

If what is of God partakes of the quality of God, what is of man partakes of the quality of man. And everything that goes into the making of church partakes of both. For church is that distinctive community in which God and man meet.

CHAPTER IV

How the Churches Think of the Church

AN ESSAY IN UNDERSTANDING

1. The "Catholic" Idea

We are faced by the stubborn fact that the churches as we find them differ profoundly in the ways they conceive of the Church. And the recognizable forms of their divided communities clearly reflect these differences in the guiding image that each church holds of itself. Each church has sought to embody what it conceives itself to be, and has succeeded at least in part.

In this respect, churches as communities of men have a likeness to individual men. For man is a creature the form of whose life is greatly shaped by his image of himself, his hope for himself, his ideal. He conceives of himself as "sporting man" or "good business man" or "artist" or "child of God," and the manner of his life is often conspicuously shaped by this guiding image. Yet that is not the whole truth. A man is not simply an idea that takes to itself a shape. He finds himself with a given shape and given traits. He belongs to a given race, a given place, a given time. The white man's color is not his own idea, nor is the black man's. And since man to be a going concern must believe in himself, justify his own existence, he has a strong disposition to rationalize his nature as he finds it, commonly to make a virtue of it.

So it is with churches. None of them in their actuality are

simply ideas that have found embodiment in history. All of them owe much to the given circumstances of their particular origins and particular life histories. "Rome" as church has received much from "Rome" as imperial city and imperial tradition. Anglicanism carries much in its inheritance that is England. It has often been observed that many American churches of the evangelistic tradition bear the marks of "the frontier." Certainly the spirit of "free enterprise" has entered deeply into American Protestantism, for good or for ill.

The distinguishing traits of the many churches are in part the product of given circumstances. Once given, the churches—that is, we humans in them—try to perpetuate and justify and rationalize, even canonize, these traits. Often it is very difficult to distinguish what is truly the expression of our creative, guiding idea and what is the *given* of which we have sought to make the best.

Having guarded ourselves, we can repeat that the ways in which the churches conceive of the Church have done much to shape their lives. All the churches are constituted of body and spirit; all the churches profess to be communities in communion with God, specifically with God revealed in Christ. But they differ in what they hold to belong essentially to the body of the Church and as to how God is related to what is outward and visible in its common life. These differences are reflected in or read into their thought and practice on all the important aspects and organs of a church's life. They are reflected in the way it deals with its faith, in its manner of worship, in the form and character of its ministry, in how it is related to the world around it, in what kind of unity it seeks or embodies.

Our task is to understand as well as we may these fundamental differences in the ways the churches think of the Church. The task is extraordinarily difficult. If we are to speak to more than the learned few, and so serve in any measure to build a wider mutual understanding, we must struggle for simplicity. But to achieve simplicity in the treatment of what is complicated and manifold is always to be liable to a false simplicity. We must take that risk.

The task calls for charity. We are dealing with differences over which men have fought for centuries, for which men have suffered and died. We cannot understand others without imaginative sympathy. To understand others whose ways are alien or, even more, threatening to our own ways requires a kind of love for our enemies by which we seek to appreciate from within how it feels to be in their position, what they live by, perhaps even what truth they apprehend to which we have been blind.

No one can be a reconciler who cannot achieve understanding of his opponent without losing his hold on the truth with which he believes himself to be entrusted. Our task is to be reconcilers.

We would involve ourselves in a bewildering catalogue if we sought to characterize all the great church families, let alone their subdivisions. At the risk of false simplicity, I shall suggest that there are three broad divisions in the way men conceive of the Church, and consequently in the way they seek to embody it.

The first of these is the view that the Church is the great society, with its essential institutions, established on the earth by God to bring men into right relations with himself and with one another under him. It is the ark of salvation, city of God, earthly aspect and embodiment of his kingly rule, which is in heaven and is to come. This is a high church view. The Church is heavily underscored. God's approach to man, and man's answering approach to God, are through the Church in its visible, institutional, official character. For the purpose of our treatment, we shall call this the "Catholic" view.

Straightway it must be confessed that to use the word "catholic" in this way is in part to misuse it. In its primitive meaning, this rightly treasured word carries the association of wholeness and inclusiveness and universality as against the partial and local and transitory. It came to designate the true and right Church as against the false, heretical, schismatic sects and churches. No actual church can wholly surrender the high claims made under the word "catholic." To use a word for wholeness to designate a type, one way of thinking and acting among other ways, is to be misleading. Yet what less misleading word can we find? Our unhappy divisions" infect the very language we must use.

The word "catholic" is especially treasured by certain churches. It has been largely surrendered to them by others. We shall, therefore, use the word to label a way of conceiving of the Church and of embodying it. This way is represented most unambiguously by the Roman church, the Orthodox churches, and those sections of the Anglican communion which are popularly called 'Anglo-catholic" or "high church." A large proportion of the professing Christians in our world live within the orbit of this viewpoint.

The second major way of conceiving of the Church is that which thinks of it as the community of those who, having received by faith the Word of God, embodied in the Bible or communicated through the Bible, live and shape their common life in obedience to that Word. God and man meet in the Word. The Church stands forever under the Bible. It is the trustee and guardian of the Book. The true churches are the churches of the Book. The Church's task is to bring to men what is given to them by God in the Book. This view is widely represented in the churches which issued from the Reformation. We might call it the view of classical Protestantism. It is represented most purely by the Lutheran churches and by the Presbyterian and Reformed churches; it is a major element in the inheritance from the Reformation of the Anglican churches; and it is a part of the inheritance of most of the churches generally called "Protestant."

The third view of the Church is that which identifies it as the fellowship of the Spirit or the community of the Perfect Way. The emphasis here is on personal experience, on the converted heart, on moral purity and the spontaneity of the Spirit-moved or Spirit-guided life, and on the immediately realized fellowship of believers in face-to-face meeting. The tendency here is to view all outward forms with suspicion—formulas of faith, forms of worship, forms of ministry and of organization. If these are admitted at all, they are purely secondary and purely instrumental to the life of the fellowship. God and man meet in the Spirit. Thi view is represented most clearly by the Friends, but it is widel held in other Christian groups which are the heirs of the recurren movements to purge the Church of all save experiential Christians and to establish it in pure inwardness.

Having sought to characterize these three viewpoints in a preliminary way, I must immediately acknowledge that they are no more than broad divisions; perhaps it would be better to say tendencies. The actual churches do not fall tidily within these groupings. One position does not wholly exclude elements o another. The Catholic position certainly finds a place of high honor for the Bible, in principle even when not in practice. I is not unconcerned with inwardness or the spirit, and it guides many to deep experience. The churches of the classical Protestant tradition carry over many catholic marks: they commonly stress the high calling and claims of the Church itself. They are cer tainly not without forms. And it is obvious that many groups which we might classify in the third category are strongly Bible centered. Yet allowing for all this awkward running together of types, I have not been able to discover any more satisfactory instrument of understanding.

Let us then take this classification and with it seek to examine in more detail the embodiments and interpretations of the Church which we find among the churches.

We shall start with what I have called the Catholic view and embodiment of the Church. Why start there? One might say, because this is the view and embodiment which is preponderant as to the number of its adherents. But the better reason is that the Catholic view is the one from which the others broke away at the time of the Reformation and subsequently, and the other views have in important measure shaped their thought and life in protest against historic Catholicism; so we must understand this before we can understand the others. We might even hazard the statement that men are naturally "catholics" and learn to be any thing else only by hard experience. That statement is certainly open to misunderstanding. Let it mean simply that we begin by believing what we are told. We normally start our lives in trusting dependence upon the communal life within which we are nurtured. We are naturally "ritualists" in the sense that we naturally express ourselves with hands and heads and faces, and expect others to do the same.

There is that in the experience of us all which can help us to understand what we might call rudimentary Catholicism. Yet to understand highly developed Catholicism sympathetically will require some considerable effort on the part of my readers. For most of you will be Protestants of one sort or another; as such you will come to the subject with long established antipathies and suspicions. We might keep in mind, therefore, that in speaking of Catholicism we are speaking of our own spiritual ancestry. For many, many centuries, Catholicism was the practically exclusive form of church in the Europe from which our own lives stem. We cannot trace our own connections in time with Christ, with the little company of disciples gathered about him, with the apostolic men who followed, with the ancient company of Israel which went before, without tracing those connections through ages of Catholicism. Whether or not we think our Catholic ancestors used rightly the treasures committed to them, they carried to us across the years the Bible, the Gospels, the words of the prophets to which we and our Protestant forebears have appealed in passing judgment on the church from which they revolted.

The Catholics in our own time, whether Roman Catholics or Eastern Orthodox, are recognizably descendants of our own forefathers. If as Protestants we judge those fathers to have erred greatly or to have sinned greatly, we are confessing the sins of our own ancestors, which might make us a little more tender. And we might even come to acknowledge that we do not wholly escape the human weaknesses we are so ready to ascribe to them.

When we look at Catholicism as embodied and expressed most clearly in the Roman Catholic Church and in the Ortho-dox churches, we find a multitude of familiar features. We must

try to see the essential features and see them in their intercon-
nectedness as part of one whole. I have suggested, without the
least claim to originality, that the key to understanding the whole
is that for Catholicism, God comes to men and men come to God
through the Church as a visible, tangible continuing institution.
The Church does for the individual, things which are essential
to him and which none other can do. She teaches him what he
could not otherwise know. She nurtures him. From her he learns
to pray. She intercedes for him. She disciplines him. She pardons
him. She is with him in sickness and at death. She is mother to
him. He is a "son of the Church." Catholics particularly treasure
and use with full naturalness the phrase "Mother Church." One
is as secure with her as in the bosom or in the womb.

Implicit in Catholic thought and practice is the idea that the
individual man does not stand alone, least of all in his life with
God. He is dependent on society. Even for God the meaning of
an individual life is not limited to what is present in the individual's
own mind and heart. Most of us in our ordinary human dealings
surely show favor to a boy because he is the son of an old friend,
or even because he graduated from the school which we attended.
The meaning of people to us is strongly conditioned by their
social context. It is natural for the Catholic to think that God
weighs the meaning and value of a life not simply as a detached
human atom but in terms of its connections. The prayers of
"Mother Church" for an erring human have weight with God,
even as we give weight to the fact that the boy who comes to us
seeking help is the son of a mother whom we love. When the
church adopts a child in baptism, that adoption carries much
weight with God, just as the adoption by my son or brother of
a child would carry much weight with me. Our relatedness enters
deeply into what we are to ourselves and to one another. The
Catholic mind works with the faith that our relatedness, especially
our relatedness to the Church, enters deeply into what we are
to God.

This Church which holds so central a place in the Catholic

mind is *holy* Church; its sacraments are holy sacraments; the Church's tradition is for Roman and Eastern Catholicism holy tradition; the pope, for Romanists, is "holy father." All these are sanctities. Which is to say that the Church in its visible, institutional character—its teachings formulated in dogma, its priesthoood and hierarchy of ministers and governors, its rites and ceremonies, its laws—partakes of the quality of God. God's presence and saving action among men are mediated through all of these. There is a strong tendency here to divinize or absolutize the visible church. Individual teachers within the Church may doubtless err from time to time, but the Church's dogma or holy tradition is inerrant. Even individual popes may err, and they are certainly sinful men, but the papacy in its loftiest functions is impeccable. Priests are failing men but the priesthood is unblemished. The Church in its ideal character is not under judgment.

The Church's authoritative teaching as embodied in ancient creeds, the decisions of councils of the Church's bishops or of her supreme bishop, is unqualifiedly God's truths, for the Catholic; therefore it is infallible, without error, not subject to change, though subject to expansion. To have faith is to believe unquestioningly what the Church authoritatively teaches. Even the Bible is the Church's book; the one true version of it is the Church's version, and the one true interpretation is the Church's interpretation. There is no appeal past the Church. One can only appeal from the Church to the Church, from priest to bishop, from bishop to council of bishops or to the supreme bishop. The ultimate decision of faith for any man is the decision to believe the Church; that decision made, all else follows; he stands now under a law of belief; it is his bounden duty to believe what the Church believes, the Church in its visible, institutional character.

There is an old distinction between "faith" in the sense of heart's trust or the affirmative answer of the whole person to God revealed in Christ, and "the faith" as the truths to be believed about God and our relations with him. These two cannot be wholly separated. There could be no faith in another person that did not carry with it by implication at least the apprehension of some truths about a person which could be put into propositions and affirmed. But simple faith as between man and man or as between man and God may be found and may be very effective even when inarticulate and unconscious of its own implications. Likewise, formal assent to the propositions of "the faith" may be found with very little evidence of "faith" in its elemental meaning.

Among the churches as we meet them, there are marked differences as to the emphasis they place on "faith" and "the faith." Catholicism places a strong emphasis on "the faith." It would not be at all fair to say that it fails to stress personal faith or the heart's trust or the will's obedience. But the proximate, immediate object of faith is the Church which teaches "the faith." The believer's faith is led through the Church to the saints, to the Blessed Mary, to the Christ and the eternal Father. The simple believer does not personally apprehend or understand all the dogmas of the faith, all the answers to all the questions which faith can ask in seeking to articulate itself. As the questions are asked, the Church answers them. The believer can be secure and protected by the assurance that the Church has the answers.

Catholicism is sacramental through and through. Its worship is most characteristically a holy action of the Church. Its seven sacraments are all viewed as instituted by God, either directly by God the Incarnate Son or indirectly by God the Holy Spirit guiding apostolic men. The Church does not talk to people chiefly; it acts upon them or for them. It takes them up into its life, as a family takes a child up into its life or a nation takes people up into its life. It embraces them; it accepts them; it banishes them; it pardons them; it intercedes for them.

These are all visible, tangible occurrences. One knows when they happen and where they happen, as one knows when and where one was adopted into a family, or married, or naturalized as a citizen, or graduated from college, or condemned by a court or pardoned by a governor, or given a commission in the army. Something was done, and done by a person who had authority to do it, and one was given something to symbolize and validate it.

And in all this, for the Catholic, God is active and present. It is not simply that these are things which God once upon a time commanded men to do, as reminders of what he once did or said. When the Church baptizes, God then and there adopts this person into the household of his Church, pardons and cleanses, and endows with a new status and power. When the Church celebrates the sacrifice at the altar, Christ descends again into man's world and again offers himself in atonement for man's sins and again so identifies himself with that which the Church blesses that in receiving what is consecrated men draw near again to the very body of Christ. When the Church banishes, God banishes; and when the Church receives again the penitent, God receives again.

The central and most characteristic act of Catholic worship, certainly of Western or Roman Catholicism, is the sacrifice of the mass. What Christ did long ago in offering his body to be broken to glorify God and in atonement for man's sins is re-enacted. The main movement of this act is from man to God. There is relatively little emphasis on communion or on God's loving giving of himself *to* men. There is little, if any, emphasis on the members of the body of Christ finding renewed fellowship with one another by union with him who is the Head of the body. The preaching of the converting Word has a small place.

In Catholicism, what God does in and through his Church is done through an official priesthood and hierarchy which serve as the human organs or agents of God. One cannot overstress the *official* character of this ministry. Priests and bishops are officers, as captains or generals in the army are officers or as governors and judges are officers of states. Whatever their personal gifts or virtues or failings, they have rank and authority, and they are under authority, ultimately God's authority.

But God's authority is mediated always through the Church. Their business is to do what it is the Church's business to do, to teach what the Church teaches. The faithful respect their rank, not their persons, as a good citizen, not too disillusioned, respects the office of the presidency or the office of a justice of the Supreme Court. They wear a uniform, to identify them as officers; and beyond that, since their most exalted function is as agents of the Church's sacramental action, they themselves partake of this sacramental character; it is given them in ordination. They are a holy priesthood; they go before God's people into the Holy of Holies, into the sanctuary; they bring holy things within men's timid reach; and as a very natural expression of all this their bodily persons are covered, in their sacramental acts, by impersonal garments symbolic of their sacramental character.

This being the nature of the Catholic ministry, the greatest pains are taken to insure that those who are to exercise it shall be commissioned by those who hold authority, and shall gain their sacramental character from those who already possess it. This ministry is no mere convenience fashioned by the Church for its own purposes. Its powers and authority do not come up from below as an expression of the democratic will of the Church's people. This priesthood is a gift of God to his Church. Its authority comes from above. Its origins are seen in Christ's empowering and commissioning of his apostles as his plenipotentiaries. The Church's bishops are the bearers of the authority and sacramental power in apostolic succession. To be without them is to lack the ministry which God in Christ has given to his Church.

Particularly within Roman Catholicism the exaltation of the priestly order has tended strongly to place the laity in the position of silent partners. They have no part in the church's government, in the selection of its leadership or in the determination of its policies. These powers center in the official hierarchy, and authority descends upon the people from above. Protestants believe that in these uncriticized powers of the priesthood lie the seeds of clericalism and the discouragement of a self-reliant laity.

There are many other marks of the Church as interpreted and embodied in its Catholic form, the most significant of which are closely related to some of those already mentioned. It is certainly marked by outwardness, an unhesitating elaboration of visible symbolism and of all that I have called the "bodily" elements of human community. All the forms of human art are freely used to glorify the places of worship, the pageantry of worship, the priesthood and the hierarchy.

Those who stand within more austere ecclesiastical traditions can best understand all this if they recognize that even in a democratic nation we seek to glorify and give impressiveness to the institutions of our national life by the architecture of courts of justice, of capitol buildings and of the presidential mansion. Our officers of state are inducted with considerable pageantry; our universities have their occasions of colorful pomp when symbols of office are carried. For the Catholic, it seems wholly suitable that the riches and beauty of God's world should be freely expended in the glorification of God in his Church and not reserved for banks and movie theaters or Greek-letter fraternities.

The Catholic puts the bodily and his body into his worship, with at least as much intelligibility as that with which the citizen salutes the flag or the child kisses his mother. He does not hesitate to bless and sanctify material things and then to find a blessing in them. To use a homely illustration suggested by a friend, do we not feel that we have participated in the marriage feast by partaking of the wedding cake or in the birthday festival by sharing in the birthday cake? And do we hesitate to take with us to an absent friend that which can make him, too, a sharer in the festival? The Catholic finds his participation in the holy by means not unlike these.

Catholicism, just because it views the Church as the institutional agent of God, is highly traditional; it guards tenaciously every symbol and guarantee of its legitimacy, of its undeniable, recognizable continuity with its own past. It has a long memory. By observances, by images, by guarding the relics of its past, it keeps alive its consciousness of community with the saints and with all the faithful of other times.

Since for Catholicism the Church is the one lawful institution authorized by God himself to bring men his saving truth and saving help, its dealings with men tend to take on a legal character, comparable with the relation of a government and the people governed. Indeed, God's own relations with men are frequently presented in legal terms. Men are subject to a law of belief, a law of worship and observance, at least a minimal law of conduct. Since law can never reach effectively behind outer behavior, the working test of a good churchman is whether he accepts what the Church says and observes what the Church requires. And the idea lies close at hand that to meet these manageable requirements is to be in good standing with God.

We may well ask whether churches that do not cherish the Catholic name are quite free from this legalism. Does the Protestant never feel that he has done his duty to God, or even gained some credit with God, simply by going to church? In any case, we can recognize that this is a mark of Catholicism and part of its effective strength. Men know quite definitely what they are expected to believe and to do, and they know whether they have done it. And by this minimum conformity they are held within the reach of that which constantly presents God's claim upon them.

For the Catholic mind, the Church is frankly a "mixed" society. It makes no claim that all its members are saints or deeply converted or pure, or have gone far in the personal understanding of Christian faith, or are destined without much purgation to find a place in God's eternal kingdom. The Church's authoritative teaching is pure truth of God. The sacraments are unfailing springs of sanctifying power. To be within the Church is to have access to this saving truth and saving power; to be outside the Church is to be cut off from them. But for those within, there are many degrees of effective participation in that which the Church brings to men from God.

In this sense, Catholicism is disposed to be tolerant, not expecting too much of men, ready to meet them where they are; appealing to them at the level where they are found; certainly not puritanical;

even hospitable, Protestants would say, to men's superstitions. But in another direction Catholicism is by nature highly intolerant. The one God-endowed legal agency of man's salvation can recognize no rival and accept no substitute. It is as unthinkable for the Catholic mind, particularly for the Roman Catholic mind, to speak of recognizing or working with another "church" as it would be for the lawful government of the United States to recognize or work with a rival government setting itself up in this country to be a true government. The situation is one of rebellion, and of rebellion against God's own representatives. Doubtless there are some very worthy people in the rebel alleged churches, but that only makes matters worse, for it lends a plausibility to them which is confusing to the faithful.

From what has been said regarding the Catholic idea of the Church, one can readily see the direction which must be taken by the Catholic idea of the unity which marks it and must be preserved or recovered. No mere spiritual unity is enough; certainly not a cooperative alliance of bodies which do not share the one articulated faith, which do not use the same sacraments and do not possess the one authoritative ministry. The Church is essentially the one great objective institution. Its unity must be objective, institutional, a visible unity of faith and order.

I have tried to characterize in broad terms some, only some, of the chief marks of the Catholic conception of the Church and embodiment of the Church. Among the actual churches or sections of churches which are commonly designated as Catholic there are of course important differences. Roman Catholicism is markedly more legal in its thought and practice than is Eastern Orthodoxy. It lays far more stress on a highly centralized governmental unity. Its dogmas are more fully and rigorously formulated; so it presents a more stringent law of belief. Its Western view of man's fallen condition is more dark and its worship carries with it a heavier stress on Christ's propitiation and man's constant need of pardon. Having passed through the experiences of the Reformation and counter-Reformation, it is deeply intrenched in its condemnation of Protestantism. Above all, it possesses in the papacy what is held to be an organ of infallible interpretation for its authoritative tradition, and what is certainly a powerful center of governmental unity across political barriers.

The Orthodox churches find their ultimate standard in a "holy tradition" which is less sharply defined than Roman dogma, more fluid and therefore more malleable. Their highest organ of interpretation is a general council of Orthodox bishops, who find it practically impossible to meet because their churches are so deeply enmeshed in nationalistic political divisions. The worship of Orthodoxy, highly formalized and ritually elaborate, centers in a sacramental celebration of the coming of the very life of God into our human life, and the resurrection victory. In spite of the high political barriers which divide them, the Orthodox churches keep extraordinarily true to type with respect to the dogmas of the faith and the order of their ministry, and above all in their liturgies. As one interpreter has put it, they are like armies in identical uniforms, marching in step with one another down parallel alleys separated by formidable walls of political division.

Just because this expression of Catholicism is less legal and less marked by governmental unity than Roman Catholicism, the churches of Orthodoxy have shown themselves more ready to give a qualified recognition to other churches and to meet and work with them in many ways. They can recognize in these other churches true elements of the "holy tradition" even though in incomplete forms, and on that basis can make common cause with them.

"Anglo-catholicism" is, by contrast with both of these, not a church but a movement within that church family which is commonly called "Anglicanism." These names, because of their similarity, are confusing to those who are outside of this church family and to many who are within it. Anglicanism is a name for the stream of church life stemming from the Church of England. Some are disposed to characterize the Anglican communion as a Protestant church with strong Catholic reminiscences, and others would describe it as a Catholic church with strong Protestant coloring. In any case, it has a decidedly mixed character.

Within this family of churches there is a vigorous movement which has come to be called "Anglo-catholicism" and which seeks to embody an Anglican version of Catholicism. It stresses and exalts the Catholic elements in the Anglican tradition; the ancient creeds as the embodiments of the Catholic faith; a sacramental emphasis, which in its more extreme form seeks to revive the seven sacraments of developed Catholicism; and most emphatically a priestly ministry secure in its apostolic authority because derived from an unfailing succession of bishops.

Anglo-catholicism has seen its natural allies in Rome and in Orthodoxy, with meager encouragement from Rome but considerable cordiality from some of the hierarchies of the politically harassed churches of the east. On the other hand, those within the Anglican household of a decidedly catholic mind have lived in constant association with fellow Anglicans of a decidedly Protestant outlook. They have breathed a freer intellectual air than is found within the two major forms of Catholicism. Consequently they are more ready to rethink the Catholic position and to search for a genuine reconciliation with the Protestant witness.

CHAPTER V

How the Churches Think of the Church
2. The Classical Protestant Idea

We turn now to a second broad way of conceiving of the Church. It is found and embodied most clearly in what I shall call, somewhat arbitrarily, classical Protestantism. Among the existing church families, the Lutheran churches and the Presbyterian and Reformed churches may be taken as the clearest examples, though the ideas and forms of church life of which we shall be thinking pervade widely most of the churches commonly called Protestant. Whereas Catholicism is found among us in only two or three major embodiments, Protestantism presents many variants. As a result, it is more difficult to characterize in a single treatment without blurring overmuch the significant differences.

Yet classical Protestantism has its great common features. The core of it is that God's Word or gospel stands forever above God's Church, that to receive the blessings of this Word there must be a real spiritual answer in the heart of the believer, that every Christian man is summoned to a responsible encounter with this Word, and that answering to this Word and testifying to it is the shared calling of the faithful in the togetherness of their common life. Protestantism is rooted in a deep disillusionment with and a moral revolt against the great institution embodying the high claims of Catholicism.

The Reformation movement from which these churches and

their Church idea issued was many-sided and assuredly not free from quite secular and even unworthy motivations. But it was certainly a *reformation* movement. Sensitive spirits recognized that the house of God was in desperate need of housecleaning. The institution which claimed to be the sole bearer of the sanctifying leaven in the world was itself widely corrupt, and therefore quite evidently corruptible. There was corruption in monasteries, which were supposedly prime centers of sanctity; there was an offensive measure of immorality in the holy priesthood; there was evident greed and will to power in high places; common opinion viewed bishops as ambitious, greedy and worldly.

Claiming inerrancy, the church was teaching, or permitting to be taught, doctrines which many devout minds judged to be religiously false. The one Mediator was obscured by a crowd of lesser mediators. The mother-church idea had reached a point where her children were held in perpetual dependence on her, and she failed to nurture them as free and responsible sons. Consecrated things were treated as though they possessed magical powers. The objective potency of sacraments was stressed to a point where the personal help of God and the movement of his Spirit could be treated as an infused power calling for a minimum of personal outreach and response. Men were permitted, even encouraged, to think that they could earn a good standing with God by good works, or even that the church through its priesthood could arrange things with God for them. Multitudes received sacramental ministration and manifested precious few signs of having received inward and spiritual help. Something must be radically wrong. The Spirit had departed widely from the institution.

In the Book which the Catholic Church acknowledged to contain the primary self-disclosure of God and the record of his redemptive dealings with men, troubled seekers found much that spoke to their condition. They found much testimony that God forever stands above the institutions and agencies which he himself has established in time to serve his purposes. His mysterious and sovereign decrees repeatedly break the patterns of men's expectations, even of those based on his own past dealings with them. He has judged priesthoods that have failed him. He has destroyed the very temple where he once met with men. He has chosen people who were not his people to be his people. His promises are fulfilled, but sometimes in ways upsetting to those who are assured that they stand in the right succession. "God is able of these stones to raise up children unto Abraham." His judgments and his mercies have repeatedly broken over the limits in which men have sought to confine him.

The God who spoke to these troubled seekers in the Book does not permit himself to be managed by men. He remains sovereign always. He demands inwardness, a trusting and obedient response within men which can come only from the free working of his Spirit in them. His promises are to the answering, outreaching, penitent, believing soul. No external conformity to laws of worship or laws of outward conduct can establish men in his favor. Certainly his favor cannot be bought nor his disfavor bought off, no matter how exalted the ecclesiastical "fixers." Before him a man must stand in the loneliness of his own responsibility. Man does not hold it in his own broken moral capacity to satisfy God or to fulfill the law of love.

Man's standing with God, his restoration to right relations with God, is something costingly conferred by God's own love. It is conferred somewhat as a failing child's status in the family is granted him, as an unwon gift by his parents' love; or as the often disloyal lover's status is granted him by the unpurchased pardon of his beloved. This forgiving, reconciling, restoring love of God has been revealed and enacted in Christ's giving of himself to men and for men. That act of sacrifice need not be repeated. It cannot be repeated. It needs only to be accepted and laid hold of in sorrowing gratitude. There supremely is God's Word to man. Man can enter into the status of a forgiven child of God only by the trusting acceptance of a meaning for God which a man can never merit by his moral achievements. But if a man will continue to listen to God's speaking and to receive the visible assurances of God's pardoning and strengthening of him, he can grow in the power to please through the communication to him of the very Spirit of the One he is most called to please.

Such thoughts as these were kindled in men's minds and flamed into utterance. The official leadership of the existing church in the main reacted defensively, as men commonly do under criticism. The bishops, as the supreme guardians of the established church, nearly everywhere rose to the defense of the order that was, and so gained the special enmity of reforming zeal. The reformers sought and found the support of this-world powers, including princes restive under imperial rule and papal exactions, and nobles greedy for church loot. Equally, Catholic authorities turned to kings and emperor to put down this rebellion.

The reforming men had no idea whatever of establishing a new church; they were seeking to recall the church to itself. There could be no new church; the only church was Christ's Church, the apostolic Church. But step by step they were driven—by stubbornness, no doubt, and self-righteousness and exaggeration and misrepresentation on both sides—to break with the actual authorities and the visible institutions of the one existing embodied church, and they were forced, as men always are in such a situation, to look behind the front of that which they rejected to something deeper back of it.

The people who talk blandly about the precious things which the reformers should have preserved, or complain about the lovely ecclesiastical furniture that was broken, have never lived through a revolution, even in their imaginations. These men were faced with an even more disturbing and radical step than that which a man faces who breaks with the long established government of his people because he is convinced that it is proving false to the very principles which gave them birth. A man in such a situation does not believe he is deserting his people to found a new people; he believes he is recalling them to the foundations of their common life.

The reforming men, faced with the massive power and prestige of the one institution which men had recognized for centuries as speaking and acting for God, desperately needed some secure standing ground. They found it in the Bible. Here was a sure record of God speaking to his people—his ancient law, the judgment given through his prophets, the gracious acts and sayings of the Incarnate Word, the testimony of apostolic witnesses. Amid all the corruption of the Church, here was something incorruptible, the Ark of the Presence. Here men could meet God with assurance. This Word was not being given to men by the Church; they were not being confronted with it. Instead, they were offered complicated rites in a language not understood by the people, often little understood by the very priests who administered the rites. Men must be given the plain speaking of God in their own tongue. That would be apostolic succession indeed, hearing with one's own ears the apostolic witness. "Faith cometh by hearing, and hearing by the Word of God."

Out of all this came the Church idea that is carried in the inheritance of those churches which are the clearest, least mixed descendants of classical Protestantism. This conception is embodied in their visible life and practice, in their formulas and confessions of faith. Read the utterances of their founding fathers and representative spokesmen; watch what they do in their churches. The shaping conception in the background will show itself even when the attending church members may understand very imperfectly why things are as they are among them.

These are churches that know themselves to stand under the Word of God in the Holy Scriptures, under an authority with a this-world embodiment distinguishable from the Church as an institution. But they know themselves to be *churches*, visible institutions with marks, indeed with many of the associations present in the Catholic idea. They are visible, recognizable communities with an ordered common life and connectedness across time and space. The Bible is not simply handed to individuals to be interpreted by them as they will. Individuals do not congregate to form the Church. The Bible is given to the Church, and the gospel contained in the Bible, and the sacraments enjoined by the gospel. The mission of the Church in its corporate nature, the mission of the priesthood of all believers, is to receive from God and to bring to men the gospel and the sacraments of the gospel. The mother-idea is not lacking in classical Protestantism, though it is certainly far less dominant. The Church receives children into its life, the congregation of Christ's flock, by baptism. It nurtures and instructs its members. When in full vigor, it may even discipline them.

Yet these churches which are the heirs of the classical Protestant tradition do not view the Church as self-authenticating. They put into the hands of their members a Book by whose standard even the Church may be weighed and judged. In the corporate memories of these churches there echo such sayings as these: "Holy Scriptures contain all things necessary for salvation"; "The Church must not ordain anything contrary to God's written Word"; "The Word had its being before the Church and is the foundation of it"; "There may be found the sure and infallible rule whereby may be tried whether the Church doth stagger or err, and whereunto all ecclesiastical doctrines have to be called to account."

Much else follows from this. This truth which the Church is to bring to men is Bible truth or gospel truth. Referring back to the distinction between "faith" and "the faith", alluded to in the previous chapter, it can be said that classical Protestantism sought to place a much heavier emphasis on the indispensable place of faith in the sense of the heart's trust and the will's responsible decision, than is found in actual Catholicism. The Word can be received only by those who answer to it with such trust. The sacraments are efficacious only for those who receive by such trust. Men must "feed on Him" in their hearts by faith. They must be summoned to a full and responsible confession of faith.

But this strong stress on personal faith did not carry with it in classical Protestantism any minimizing of "the faith" as an objective body of truths about God and man. These churches held fast to the ancient Catholic creeds and the formulations of ancient Catholic church councils. These were sound embodiments of Bible truth, and as such were to be treasured by a faithful church. But the ancient creeds did not speak clearly on many of the questions with which the Reformation confronted the believer. So these churches formulated their own confessions of faith to articulate more fully for men that Bible truth to which the Church is committed. These were to guide the teacher and to instruct the faithful. They were far more extensive and elaborate than the old Catholic creeds. Rejecting Catholic "tradition," the reformers and their successors fashioned thus a tradition of interpretation. These creeds could and did become in their turn a law of belief as burdensome to the simple man as that from which they had sought to deliver him. Yet it must be said for the classical Protestant law of belief, as for the Catholic law of belief, that they have been to the rarely devout and instructed what the old Jewish law was to the Pharisee: "Thy word is a lamp unto my feet, and a light unto my path"; "O how I love thy law."

Guided by their fidelity to the Bible, the churches which embody the classical Protestant idea have undertaken to bring to men the sacraments of the gospel. There are two, not seven, though other edifying rites of apostolic origin might be retained. These two are still sacraments, and so named. They are strengthening means of help from God to man. They are outward and visible signs of inward and spiritual grace. But grace is no longer an infused power carried within the sacramental means as an effect is carried within its cause. They are God's gracious Word made visible, or the seal which gives full assurance to the Word, as the seal on an official document validates it.

In particular, the form and meaning of the supreme sacrament have been much changed. No human priesthood can offer Christ in sacrifice. He alone can offer himself. That he has done on earth and forever does in heaven. Faithful men can remember that sacrifice once made, and celebrate it. They can receive its benefits by faith and then offer their spiritual sacrifice of praise and thanksgiving and self-dedication. This celebration is ever incomplete without receiving. Communion is an essential part of it. Did not Christ bid men, "Take, eat"? Only those who have received in faith can make an acceptable offering. They can offer to God only what they have first accepted from him, as a son can offer his father only the sonship his father has first conferred on him in love.

When we enter a church which stands clearly within the inheritance of classical Protestantism, the Bible is in the center—often the book itself. The Word is read, not in any ancient unknown tongue, not as a ritual act, but read to be understood. And the Word is interpreted in the words of a living and contemporary man, who because he is presumed to know the Word and know the people may be expected to make the Word live for the people. Song and prayer are the people's answer to the Word.

That is the classical Protestant *idea*, often much obscured by choir solos in the concert manner and long prayers by the preacher which may suggest that he is praying at them instead of leading them in their answer to God. The Church is here conceived of as brought into being and continually re-created by hearing the Word and responding to it with faith. Sacraments there are, but they are subordinated. For the Protestant would say, "Is not the word the most effectual medium of communication between person and person, even between divine Person and human person? Without the word that carries understanding to answering faith, do not sacraments deteriorate readily into hocus pocus?"

The ministry within classical Protestantism stands like the Church itself under the sovereign Word. Its supreme task is to proclaim the gospel and to administer the sacraments of the gospel and to shepherd the faithful. This ministry is still an official ministry. It is no vagrant exercise of purely private gifts. Since the Church in its corporate character has been given the gospel and the gospel sacraments, the Church must provide a ministry fully authorized to administer this trust. Catholics are tempted to say that whereas their ministry comes "from above," this Protestant ministry comes "from below," bearing man's authority, not God's or Christ's. That is surely not the classical Protestant *idea*. The minister is ordained to be a servant of the Word. He comes to the people with and under that authority.

In Catholicism, the Church tends to be identified with the hierarchy and the priesthood it ordains. The hierarchy selects and ordains and sends the priesthood. The faithful simply receive them and their instructions and ministrations, as silent partners. In Protestantism, because of its recovered sense of the priesthood of all believers and of the trusteeship in which all the faithful share, the people through their representatives commonly share in the selection and calling of the ministry, though the authority to minister the gospel is normally given by those who already possess that authority. When the realization of the authority of the Word grows dim, this ministry can easily come to be thought of as no more than the setting apart of men to do what the church people want done.

The ministry within Catholicism is relatively impersonal and anonymous. Every priest performs the same rite in a recognizably identical manner. It does not matter too much who he is or even what are his personal gifts, so long as he gives no grave offense. But the preaching ministry and the ministry of free prayer and of highly personal pastoral relationships are qualified throughout by the individuality of the ministers, their insight, gifts of utterance, character and personality. The strengths and weaknesses of these two types of ministry are obvious.

Classical Protestantism has not in the main viewed the form of the ministry—whether of several orders or of one, whether ordained by bishops or by presbyters—as a prime essential of the Church. The churches of this tradition for the most part have been ready to recognize and accept any duly authorized gospel ministry, though the effort has often been made to reproduce forms of ministry and of church government conforming to what was believed to be the pattern of the New Testament church.

Thus far we have spoken of common elements in the Church idea and Church embodiment of classical Protestantism, and have dealt with it as though it were a unity. The fact is that in spite of these common elements it is divided within itself, though conscious of its unity and struggling to express it. The reformers and their followers shared the sincere conviction that no competent and earnest reader could fail to find in Scripture what they themselves found there. We moderns must view this as a pathetically naïve confidence. For apart from critical questions as to the original text and the historicity of the records, which did not trouble the men of the sixteenth century, it is hardly evident to us that the Bible is capable of only one interpretation by devout and honest men. We can see, unless we have been quite shut up in a single tradition of interpretation, that Luther's reading and Calvin's reading and the reading of the Anglican reformers all began quickly to diverge. And since the Bible in its entirety was hardly a manageable stand- ard, the practical result was that the Bible according to Luther or according to Calvin or according to the ruling authorities in the reformed Church of England became in effect the operative norm.

All agreed that the Church is to live under the Word and to bring the pure Word to men. But Luther was much less of a literalist in his interpretation of the Word than was Calvin. For Luther, the Word was supremely the gospel of God's pardoning love in Christ to which all the words lead but which is not found equally in all the words. For Calvin, the words all carried the full authority of God. Luther held that the Church was free to carry on good and edifying usages and institutions not expressly forbidden by Scripture. So Lutheranism carried over many of the liturgical treasures of the older Catholicism, much of its cere- monial richness and, in Sweden, the Catholic institution of episcopacy without the typically Catholic meaning. But Calvin held that the Church must do nothing that is not enjoined by Scripture, and so handed on a tradition of rigorism and austere simplicity that has characterized the churches which have particu- larly borne the mark of his influence. Luther found in Scripture no indication that a particular form of ministry or type of church government was a divine institution. So the churches of the

Lutheran tradition show much diversity in ministry and government, asking only for a duly authorized ministry. Calvin, however, found equality of ministers, pastors, teachers, ruling elders in the New Testament, and held that the Church should perpetuate the New Testament model.

The reformed Church of England came through the Reformation turmoil with the ancient Catholic institutions of bishops and the threefold orders of ministers. Its most vocal reforming leaders were convinced that this was the ancient, even the apostolic order. But they did not hold that episcopacy and these orders of ministers were divinely established essentials of the Church. They shared the common view of classical Protestantism that the essentials of the Church are present where one finds pure preaching of the Word, the two sacraments of the gospel rightly administered, and a duly authorized ministry. When, however, the Presbyterians condemned the episcopal system and held up against it the presbyterian scheme as alone bearing God's approval, Anglicans looked at the Bible again and widely came to the conclusion that bishops, priests and deacons were a divine institution, belonging in perpetuity to the essence of the Church.

Those of us who stand within the Reformation inheritance must confess that once the single overarching conciliar system of the church in the West was repudiated, and when in spite of all efforts no effective organ of common council was established, so that men of many nations were not held together in their task of interpretation, the commonly acknowledged authority of Scriptures did not hold these reformed churches to a common line.

There is another major factor in the background of classical Protestantism which bears directly on the divisions it now presents to us. The Reformation movement coincided with and was in part an expression of a wider political and social realignment in the whole Western world. I refer, of course, to the rise of nationalism, to the awakening of the claims and rights and precious values of the parts, of the local human groupings, as against the domination of the whole. As men were restive in the political sphere under the imperial system, they were restive in the church under the imperial claims of the papacy. So in the place of the international unity of Western Catholicism the characteristic unit of the new church order was the kingdom, the principality or the self-governing city.

If I may take as an example the greatest interpreter of the Anglican tradition in its first formative period, listen to Richard Hooker, writing at the close of the sixteenth century:

"For the preservation of Christianity, there is not anything more needful than that such as be of the visible Church have mutual fellowship and society one with another." But: "As the main body of the sea, being one, yet within divers precincts hath divers names; so the Catholic Church is in like sort divided into a number of distinct societies, every one of which is termed a church within itself."[1]

Hooker agreed that "dissimilitude in great things . . . draws great inconveniences after it." But the way to prevent it was not, he thought, "the yielding up of superior power over all churches in one only pastor's hands." He was too aware of what he calls "those woeful inconveniences whereunto the state of Christendom was subject heretofore, through the tyranny and oppression of that one universal Nimrod who alone did all."[2] Hooker's optimistic hope, characteristic of classical Protestantism, was that if only all the governmentally independent territorial churches would submit themselves to the one law of the Scriptures, they would keep step in matters essential even under several dominions. Can we deny the evidence of history that distinct societies which possess no strong organ of common council and few clearly shared symbols of communal allegiance, tend to draw apart, and that "mutual fellowship" becomes very tenuous?

There is yet another element in the Church idea of classical Protestantism which has done much to shape the forms of these churches and must not be neglected in our presentation. It appears

---

[1] *Works,* I, 351.

[2] *Ibid.,* III, 366.

in the formal definition of the Church which they carry in their traditions. In this definition, the Church is commonly spoken of as the "company of saints," the "congregation of true Christian believers," the "multitude of men chosen of God," the "elect of all ages." In the Lutheran tradition, the emphasis is on faith and the faithful. In Calvinistic or Reformed tradition, the emphasis is on the hidden election or choice of God.

If Protestantism is the product of a deep disillusionment regarding the outward and visible institution, it is a product too of a struggle to recover the inward reality, the hidden spirit in the being of the Church. Faith in its deepest meaning is invisible. Profession of faith men can verify, but no man can discern with full assurance the depth of another's faith. The mystery of God's secret workings in a human life is not something we can control or foresee or infallibly verify. Yet without the heart's faith and without the secret working of God, all outwardness is vain.

When therefore men seek to recover the inwardness of the Church, the Church itself threatens to disappear from sight. This problem lies close at hand in the classical Protestant definition. It is explicitly recognized in frequent references to "the visible Church" as something contrasted with "the invisible Church" or the invisible aspect of the Church.

As we have already noted, Catholicism fully recognizes and accepts the mixed character of the Church. Augustine in the fourth and early fifth centuries, whose rich, many-sided mind did so much to shape the thought of Western Catholicism—and also to feed the minds of the reformers—wrestled with this problem. He recognized that there were many in outward communion with the church who were not among the chosen of God, and even that some who seemed to be outside the church were really within it. Accordingly, he distinguished in the existing church as men actually experience it a true body of Christ and a feigned or mixed body. This did not lead him to the position that there are two churches, or to question the rightfulness of giving the name of Church to the one visible, hierarchical institution. Without achieving complete clarity or consistency, he viewed the inner kernel of true Christians as part of the larger whole.

The idea of the Church as a community of saints or true believers was not, of course, obliterated in medieval Catholicism. It was appealed to by devout spirits as the ideal to which the church was called, and by rebels to justify their separation from the existing institution. But in the main these ideas were subordinated to the thought of the church as the recognizable bearer to men of sacramental help and the supreme authority in doctrine and morals. For Catholicism, the "faithful" are those who maintain a right relation with the one authoritative church.

The Protestant movement brought with it a vigorous revival of this latent contrast between the Church as invisible and the Church as visible. Luther, in line with his whole stress on faith, taught that the Church in its deepest nature is a community of the faithful, by which he meant the whole company of those who answer with the heart's trust to God's pardoning, outreaching love in Christ. Since faith in this meaning is invisible, the company of the faithful is in a sense invisible. The human community of the faithful cannot justify itself before God or men by its own achieved perfection of faith or goodness; its true life is hid with Christ in God. But it is necessarily linked with that visible society in which the Word is preached and the sacraments of the gospel are administered. For on the one hand, faith is the answer called out by the true preaching of the Word; there can be no company of the faithful, then, save where the Word is preached. And on the other hand, the faithful will declare themselves in the preaching of the Word and observance of the sacraments, even though many feigned believers join themselves to the true and are outwardly indistinguishable from them.

But it was the visible Church, the organ by which God brings grace and redemption to men, that Luther set out to reform by bringing it back to what he saw as its primary task, the preaching of the Word which brings forth faith. Luther could not reform the invisible society of the faithful, and that society was by definition in no need of reform.

Calvin reached very similar conclusions in slightly different terms. His mind was so filled with the sense of God's mysterious secret workings and with the conviction that man could do no good thing save as God in his sovereign power willed to make that possible, that he identified the Church in its deepest nature with God's chosen. But again, this invisible number of the elect is to be found within the visible society in which true scriptural teaching and scriptural sacraments are maintained and in which there is, further, a church discipline and order conforming to Christ's institution. Where these visible means are present, God's chosen are sure to be, mingled with unconverted men, because the saving means instituted by God are never without fruit.

So classical Protestantism carries in its inheritance a deep awareness of the distinction between the inwardness of the Church and its outwardness. The two do not fall apart, but they readily could. And just because Protestantism was born out of a struggle to recover inwardness, it is marked in many ways by a stress on conscious faith, on informed decision, on the responsible participation of the lay members of the Church in its life and witness, on realized fellowship in the worshiping congregations. With all its recognition of the invisibility of faith and of the communion of the saints, Protestantism has tried—and with an important measure of success—to make the invisible more visible. In spite of all its failures, it seems fair to say that classical Protestantism has laid a heavier moral demand on the average church member than is characteristic of Catholicism. Protestants are disposed, with some deceptive pride no doubt, to see a connection of cause and effect in what appears to them the moral vigor of communities in which Protestantism has been a strong leaven, as compared with those in which Catholicism has had almost exclusive sway.

CHAPTER VI

How the Churches Think of the Church

3. The Fellowship of the Spirit or the Community of the Perfect Way

The third way of conceiving of the Church represents the carrying further of elements within classical Protestantism. The movements in history which have been most markedly shaped from within by this third Church idea began as the more radical accompaniments of the Reformation revolt against Western Catholicism or have been the result of subsequent revolts within the communities of classical Protestantism. They carry in their traditions that devotion to the sacred Book which has been so fundamental in all forms of Protestantism. They have carried even further the stress on personal faith and inwardness, on the direct access of each individual to God, on the priesthood of all believers and their realized fellowship with one another, on the freedom of the Christian man and the freedom of every local congregation of Christian people. Many would hold that these movements embody the full logic of the Protestant position.

If it is more difficult to characterize in a single treatment the actual embodiments of classical Protestantism as compared with those of Catholicism, the Church conceived as the fellowship of the Spirit or the community of the perfect way is still more difficult to gather together in idea or in fact. As we consider in turn our several types, we find increasing diversity; the process of fragmentation is progressively more apparent. This is surely no accident of history. It arises out of the very nature of the movements and of the Church ideas at work within them.

In an important measure this increasing diversity and fragmentation is bound up with the highly personal character of the movements to which we are now turning our thought. Catholicism is by comparison relatively impersonal or anonymous. The historian can isolate the contribution of creative personalities to the ongoing development of Catholicism, but the individual contributions are all absorbed into the massive and complex life of a great society. Even within classical Protestantism, where the continuing influence of a Luther or a Calvin is so clear, the variants are in the interpretation of an objectively embodied tradition. To a far greater degree, at least, the churches and groups of our third division reflect the individuality of their founders; they are more recognizably the "lengthening shadow of a man," though always of a man struggling to recover the original meaning and power of a great inheritance.

When we look out upon the totality of Christian people as found in our world, we see many groups, small and large, which do not conform to either of the types with which we have been concerned thus far. In varying measure, they are marked by ways of thought about the Church and by ways of ordering their common life which distinguish them. Some of them do not characteristically speak of themselves as churches.

As more familiar examples, we could take the "Religious Society of Friends" or a number of groups which call themselves the "Brethren." These names, "Friends" or "Brethren," are highly significant. Plainly they are reminiscent of language and feeling found in the New Testament. When compared with the major embodiments of Catholicism or the great families of classical Protestantism, these groups are often very small and are found in a confusing multitude of expressions. But surely any who carry in their sacred inheritance the Lord's word to this "little flock" and the apostolic testimony that God chooses the weak things to confound the mighty cannot speak lightly of that which is small.

In addition to these smaller societies, which are the clearest examples of the type of thought and life we are now seeking to identify, there are Christian bodies with millions of members which manifest in their forms and ways many of the marks of the little societies. These bodies frequently reserve the word "church" for the local congregation of worshiping believers and prefer to speak of their more inclusive fellowship and organization in terms of association. Typical of these in the United States are the Baptist churches, associated in the Northern Baptist Convention, the Southern Baptist Convention and the National Baptist Convention, with a combined membership in this country of some ten millions; the Disciples of Christ; the Congregational and Christian Churches. These great communions all combine in perplexing ways many of the traits of the smaller sects with the characteristics of classical Protestantism. As has already been said, this is to be explained historically by the fact that they stemmed from churches of that type and carried over much from that inheritance, as classical Protestantism had in its turn carried over much from Catholicism. Or, starting as intimate little communities of the Spirit, these movements became so large and established as to take on again the character of more conservative churches.

The great Methodist churches are particularly difficult to locate in terms of the scheme of interpretation. They are rooted in a passionate struggle for the recovery of inwardness and for Christian perfection within the widely conventionalized and widely spiritless Anglicanism of the eighteenth century. When these societies which were conceived within the body of an older church broke away from the parent body, they took with them many of the institutional forms of their inheritance. So Methodism bears many of the marks of the strong stream of classical Protestantism within Anglicanism. Yet all of its outer forms have been deeply impregnated by the spirit and ways of the church type we are now describing.

Shaping the thought and life of these little groups and these great communions in many forms and in many degrees has been the conviction that the Church in its deepest nature is truly the fellowship of the Spirit or the society of those fully committed to the perfect way set before men in the Gospels. Catholicism and classical Protestantism both find the medium of God's approach to men in something objectively presented to men; the one in the sacramental institution, the other most characteristically in the Word that speaks through the Scriptures and in the body of truths and ordinances which the Church receives from Scripture. Where these are, there is the Church. To be of the Church is to be publicly related to these, to have recognized rights of access to them, as to be of a nation is to have the privileges of citizenship. These objective institutions, these sacraments and this priesthood, these confessions of faith and ordered ministries, are powerful binders. They hold together in unity people of many temperaments and opinions, people of diverse races and social conditions. They span space and time. They hold the generations together.

Alike in Catholicism and in classical Protestantism the tragic fact is recognized, however sadly or complacently, that there will be many degrees of inward participation and responsiveness within the visible Church. It is a mixed, and in that sense an impure, society. But where these knowable institutions are, there is the Church with its means of grace or its saving gospel. The truth of God is there, either as the Church's inerrant dogma or as the sure truths of Scripture articulated by the Church. The Ark of Salvation stands; the leaven works; little children are brought in infancy to be nurtured within the household of the true faith; they are brought up in the citizenship which is their true birthright. The ministry is there, either as the authoritatively ordained priesthood or as the ordered ministry which, whatever its personal failings, brings to men the objective truths of Scripture.

So it is quite compatible with the genius of both Catholicism and classical Protestantism, when conditions are favorable, to reach out and seek to identify themselves with the whole com-

munity within which the Church stands. They have allied themselves with friendly governments, and have thus sought to permeate
the common life of a nation with God's truth and to make available
to all the Word and the sacraments. However alien this is to our
American tradition, we can see it happening not only in Catholic
countries but in Lutheran Sweden or in Calvinistic Geneva or in
Elizabethan England.

As we have already observed, there is that in classical Protestantism which points in another direction, and which if followed further
could readily lead to another position. It is the Church conceived
as the company of the truly faithful or the chosen of God and
the fellowship of the saints; it is the struggle for the recovery of
manifest inwardness and for purity of faith and life; it is the
attempt to make the invisible more visible. When these thoughts
and strivings revive and break free from old moorings, where do
they lead? They lead in diverse directions according to what are
taken to be the surest evidences of interior faith or the clearest
marks of saintliness and purity of life.

The Church is the company of the truly faithful. But faith is
no docile acquiescence in a creed and faithfulness is no conven-
tional reception of sacraments. It is the enthusiastic "Yes" of the
heart and will to the reality of God and to the wonder of his love
for sinners, manifested in Christ. Such faith is communicative;
it testifies; it gladly bears witness. Let the Church be made up of
those who have been granted the gift of such self-evidencing faith.
Let each man stand upon his feet and bear his witness in his own
language concerning what the Lord has done and means to him.
The faithful will recognize one another when they speak face
to face of a shared experience.

It is playing with words to talk about the faith of an infant; no
man can stand sponsor for another's faith. Every man must make
his own decision of faith. Was it not so in the first pure years of
the Church, disclosed to us in the New Testament? Let us return
past all the corruptions of history to those first pure years. Men
cannot be made answerable to God by being handed sacred sub-

stances or by being told to repeat man-made words, but only by the movement of God's Spirit in their hearts. The faithful may then declare their faith by submitting before men to the ordinances of God; they may go down bodily into the waters of baptism in token that they have by God's grace put off the old man and put on the new; they may break the bread of fellowship and receive the cup in token that they do receive with faith the benefits of Christ's atoning death.

The Church is the fellowship of the saints. The saints are converted men. They have been delivered from the bondage of enslaving passions and from the service of themselves. They may even know the day and the hour when their release came and when they began to walk in newness of life. Are there not decisive battles in the inner world as in the outer world, when men know that the victory has been won even though there is still much mopping up to do? The saints have turned from the vanities of the world, its pomp and pride, its pagan pleasures, its compromises, its legalism, its violence. They do not dance, for dancing is an occasion for lust; they do not drink; they do not game. The saints do not take oaths; their yea is yea and their nay, nay. The saints dress simply. There is none who is master among them, for One is their Master and all they are brethren. The saints do not go to law; they do not commit violence; they do not make war, for they know themselves called to the way of perfectness. Let the Church be made up of these, of "the worthiest, be they never so few." Let it be a fellowship of converted men who can bear convincing testimony to their own deliverance. Let it be a comradeship of those committed to the way of perfectness and ready to walk in it.

The movements we are seeking to describe and not only to describe but to appreciate—do not combine within themselves all these interpretations of the marks of the converted man or all these identifications of the demands of the perfect way. But they all share the note of deep moral seriousness, this puritan strain. They understand from within those gospel words: "If ye were of the world, the world would love his own; but because ye are not of the world, but I have chosen you out of the world, therefore the world hateth you"; "They are not of the world, even as I am not of the world."

The Church is the fellowship of the Spirit. God moves inwardly in its members; they go down deep into the silence, and there in the hidden depths he speaks. What the Spirit declares, they utter; no liturgical responses, no formalized confession, but the Spirit's utterance. What need have they of baptism with water who have been baptized with the Spirit? What need of outward means of communion for those who have been granted such deep communion in the Spirit? *Concern* God gives them—concern which they share with one another for the world's hunger and the world's injustice and the world's brutality, concern like his who looked on the multitude and had compassion.

The faithful, the converted, the saints, the Spirit-led, draw together; they delight to congregate. In the meeting of the faithful they can share their testimony, their spontaneous prayers, their concern. They find this fellowship in the face-to-face meeting of the congregation within the meetinghouse. There in the congregation of the faithful the Church is really found. For where Christ is, there is the Church, and the focus of his presence in the Spirit is now found, certainly not in the sacrament of the altar, not even so vividly in the Word, but in the gathered fellowship itself.

There is a quality of fellowship here quite foreign to Catholicism and not characteristic of the larger congregations of classical Protestantism. The congregation at a Catholic mass is by contrast anonymous, with the democracy of anonymity, all equal in the presence of the mystery but with no expectation of personal sharing, let alone of spontaneous utterance. The fellowship of the Spirit at its best is something radically different. It is hardly achieved save in a small intimate group marked throughout by personal acquaintance, though efforts are made to maintain the quality in larger congregations. The congregation is "sociable." It has a family quality. The reticence of men with one another is broken through. Even when a member of such a church moves or travels to another neighborhood, he searches out his spiritual kindred and expects to be taken into the family. This is no doubt an idealized account, but it describes the "guiding image" which is at work where the Church is predominantly conceived as the fellowship of the Spirit.

Listen to that modern Friend, Thomas R. Kelly, bear his witness to the "blessed community":

"When we are drowned in the overwhelming seas of the love of God, we find ourselves in a new and particular relation to a few of our fellows. The relation is so surprising and so rich that we despair of finding a word glorious enough and weighty enough to name it. The word *fellowship* was discovered, but the word is pale and thin in comparison with the rich volume and luminous bulk and warmth of the experience which it would designate. For a new kind of life-sharing and of love has arisen, of which we have had only dim hints before. Are these the bonds of love which knit together the early Christians, the very warp and woof of the Kingdom of God? In glad amazement and wonder, we enter upon a relationship which we had not known the world contained for the sons of men. Why should such bounty be given to unworthy men like ourselves?"[1]

Many and various are the forms and expressions of those movements of the inward Spirit. Some stress conversion, definitely experienced; some, silent waiting for the Spirit's utterance. Adult commitment as a basis for membership, the covenant of members with one another in a "gathered" church, rigor of moral demand, longing for holiness, a striving to return to the simplicity of the primitive church, a preference for spontaneity, a fear and resentment of form, a non-sacramental worship, an informal ministry or no ministry at all, greater or less withdrawal from the involvements of civil government—all these are expressions of this third conception of the Church.

---

[1] Thomas R. Kelly, *A Testament of Devotion* (New York: Harper & Brothers, 1941), p. 77.

Let us consider a little further how this Church idea re-shapes characteristically some of the major elements in a church, which are found in other forms within Catholicism and classical Protestantism.

Wherever a church is found, one finds men wrestling with the deep questions presented by "faith" and "the faith." For Catholicism, "the faith" is clearly a possession of the Church, embodied authoritatively in its creeds and dogmatic decisions. The individual believers and the local congregations of believers stand always under this authority. For classical Protestantism, the Bible is the one supreme "rule of faith." But this final standard of right teaching is entrusted to the Church in its corporate capacity as into the hands of a great corporate body of trustees. The Church as a whole, the Lutheran Church or the Presbyterian Church, formulates its apprehension of the truth of God as given in the Scriptures. No claim is made that these formulations are inerrant or not subject to change. But the responsibility for interpretation resides in the total Church. The Bible is made available to the individual believers and to the local congregations, but these in fact are held within the frame of the Church's common confession. Personal confession of faith is stressed, yet the Church brings to a man the answers to its own questions.

The movements we are now seeking to describe have shared in many degrees a strong aversion to all "human creeds." In part this aversion has been based on the fact that creeds and confessions are "formal." Being formal, they can readily be received quite formally. Their acceptance or public utterance carries no guarantee of the heart's trust or of saving experience. These movements search for the guarantee of the Spirit's presence and of the heart's trust.

In large measure this aversion to creeds has been based on the judgment that they are "human." No human, fallible form of words must stand between a man and God's Word. The Bible must be placed directly in the hands of each man and then God's truth can lay hold of him and he can lay hold of it. The Church, even as responsible trustee, must not stand between men and God. For the Church is the gathering together of those who have been laid hold of directly by God's Word.

It would be quite false to say that these movements have had among them no traditions of interpretation. No church ever lives without such. They have been guided and kept true to type by a living, oral tradition of interpretation carried by their ministries, often carried in their hymns, but carried too, as among the Friends, in the fellowship itself. The Baptist reads his Bible with a Baptist's eye as the Catholic with a Catholic eye and the Friend with a Friend's eye. There is no escape from a tradition of interpretation. If Catholic creeds and classical Protestant confessions are forever in danger of formalism, oral traditions of interpretation are highly vulnerable, too; they can become very thin. They are very subject to the vagaries of private interpretation. A price is paid for every particular value purchased in this world.

Wherever a church is found, one finds prayer and worship, for a church is a community of prayer and worship. In Catholicism, worship is plainly an act of the church in its official, priestly character. It is something objectively enacted in dramatic form. The individual worshiper attends, hears and from time to time is asked to make his own response by word or act as an expression of the fact that he is party to this which the priest does at the altar. There God is renewing his coming to men, and the church is renewing its meeting with God. The individual joins his own prayers to the prayers of the church, commonly in a form of words which the church teaches him. If he be a true worshiper, he secretly brings his own "intentions" and makes his own personal applications.

In the worship of classical Protestantism the church as trustee of the Word brings that Word to men through its ordained ministry. The Word is read and interpreted by one who bears the commission of the whole church to interpret. On particularly solemn occasions, the church through its ministry brings to its people the sacrament in which the Word is made visible and sealed, and they are bidden to receive together in faith. To all of this the people together and individually are asked to make their responses in hymns and prayers.

No sharp line can be drawn between the tradition of worship in classical Protestantism and the tradition in the churches of our third division. Yet the increasing stress on immediately felt experience is evident. Spontaneity and informality are highly valued, and therefore the temptation is present to simulate them when they cannot be achieved. An effort is made to recover and constantly to renew the original enthusiasm. The convert gives his testimony. In the prayer meeting the faithful share with one another their own stumbling prayers. Worship is here most characteristically the shared expression of what is inwardly felt and apprehended by the gathered worshipers.

The sacraments become ordinances or disappear. Baptism is no longer a holy action of the church toward the one baptized, bearing within it the blessing and the cleansing power of God. It is primarily an act of faithful obedience on the part of the believer, wherein he testifies publicly to his faith and to the gift of new life which he has already received. The Lord's Supper is primarily an act of fellowship in which the congregation of believers testifies together in act to that communion in the Spirit which is already theirs.

No church—indeed no continuing form of human society—exists without leadership. Leadership to be effective always possesses some authority in however elementary a form. To be a leader one must have the power to gain a following, to be listened to, to be believed, to make decisions and perform acts which others accept. Because a church is a community gathered about God as its center, with Christ as its head, the essential leadership in a church is concerned with the relations between God and his people. Where we find a church, we find those who speak for God to his people, or speak for his people toward God; who go before his people in the following of that way which they believe to be God's way.

The sources of authority and the ways in which it is acquired are many. We may accept a doctor's diagnosis and prescription because his confident manner inspires trust or because he has a license to practice or holds a degree in medicine. We obey a policeman's signal not because of any personal qualities in the man but because he is a policeman. A governor's pardon is effective not because he is a forgiving man but because he is a governor. When a king of England is crowned, the meaning of that man for that people is profoundly changed. His powers of making decisions which bind others are very slight but his symbolic meaning is a powerful fact. So the authority which makes leadership effective within any special human group may be derived from personal qualities, from public recognition, from legal status, or from the communication to a person of symbolic meaning.

We have seen that within Catholicism the ministry is unmistakably official and sacramental. This corresponds with the whole nature of Catholicism. God's authority is ultimate here as it must be in any church. But God's authority is embodied in the church's dogmas and the church's law. His sanctity is communicated to the church's most solemn acts. So those who declare and interpret the dogma, those who administer the law, and above all those who officiate in the sacred acts, must possess unmistakable authority and must be given the meaning of sacred personages. Where Catholicism is in vigorous spiritual health, care is taken that those who are to be given this position shall be reasonably consecrated men with a consciousness of vocation. Care is taken, too, that they shall be well instructed in the church's dogma and law and sacramental practice. But none of these makes a man a priest or a bishop. That authority and that sacramental character are conferred in ordination. The man's personal character is not changed by that act; his learning is not increased; but his meaning for the faithful is profoundly changed, and in the Catholic view his meaning for God is changed too, since God stands by the acts of his church. Ordination is here comparable alike with the commissioning of officers of state and with the coronation of a king.

We have seen that within classical Protestantism the ministry is still strongly official but its sacramental character is far less marked than within Catholicism. Again, this corresponds with the nature of classical Protestantism. God has committed to his church in its corporate capacity his gospel and the sacraments of the gospel. He has ordained that his church shall maintain a ministry solemnly charged with the authority to bring to men gospel truth and the gospel sacraments. Within the churches of classical Protestantism this authority is given in ordination, and it is recognized within the whole church in which it is conferred. Due care is presumably taken that the man is himself answerable to the gospel he is to preach, and learned in the truths of Scripture as the church has received them. Since sacraments are here predominantly interpreted as declaratory acts adding God's seal to his Word, rather than as instruments of sanctifying power, ordination is thought of as conferring authority to administer God's seals as well as to proclaim the church's gospel. It does not confer symbolic, sacramental meaning on the man ordained.

When we turn to the churches of our third type we can observe that a change takes place in the thought and practice regarding the ministry which is in line with the other tendencies we have noted. Here we meet with an emphatically "plain-clothes" ministry that reflects the falling away of the idea of the minister as an officer with the authority of rank and of the idea of him as a man with symbolic meaning. In the more extreme cases we find no official ministry.

The distinction between the ordained and the unordained is far less clear even when present. For these are seeking to be churches of the Spirit. The Spirit as a personal possession and the interior gifts of the Spirit cannot be conferred by ritual act or solemn commissioning. No bishop and no presbytery can confer enthusiasm for Christ or gifts of eloquent testimony or moral insight, or a sensitive conscience or a converted will. These are direct gifts of God. They may well be granted more evidently to the lay person than to the minister. They cannot be hired and paid for. The most that the fellowship of the Spirit can do or should do is to recognize these gifts where they are given, to welcome them and encourage their exercise. Perhaps a local fellowship, finding such gifts in one of their number, should license him to minister among them or even certify to other congregations of the faithful that this one is spiritually qualified to carry on a ministry of the Spirit. His authority does not come from the church or through the church. Should not he who is convincingly indwelt by the Spirit be set free to minister in all things spiritual? What matter whether he be learned or unlearned? What could a license or a commission or a title add? Should not he that has the gifts of healing, heal? Should not he that has the gifts of judging, judge? Should not he that has the gifts of commanding, command?

These are the directions in which the thought and practice regarding the Church's ministry move within the communities of the type we are now considering. In practice these tendencies are much qualified by the inheritance from more conservative Protestantism, so that what we actually find is in the main minglings of these two ideas: the idea of the Spirit-endowed man and the idea of the man commissioned by the Church to preach the gospel committed to it.

There are still other manifestations of our third idea of the Church which should be noted, however briefly. And in noting them we shall not exclude all criticism. For if Catholicism and classical Protestantism have their failings and even corruptions, so have the churches that have sought what they conceive to be the perfect way.

Because the Church is here found most unmistakably in the congregations of the faithful, these churches are strongly "congregational" in the ordering of their life and fearful of all overarching or centralized authority. The representatives of the lay membership are granted large powers in the selection of the ministry, in the admission of new members, in discipline and in church government. With this congregationalism there can readily come a spirit of local independence that loses a feeling for the organic quality of the Church as indeed "one body." And with the democratic procedure there may well come a forgetting that the Church forever stands under a kingly authority before which men are called to bow.

One of the most precious values of the churches of the Spirit is the Christian brotherliness of the congregation and the personal sharing of the intimacies of Christian experience. But it must be acknowledged that the very effort to achieve within a congregation a social unity comparable with a company of friends may threaten to turn the church into a company of naturally congenial people. At their best, the fellowships of the Spirit have actualized again the truth that in Christ there is neither male nor female, Jew nor Gentile, bond nor free. But the churches which have placed the strongest emphasis on the realized fellowship of the congregation have also shown the greatest tendency to reflect the natural groupings of congeniality among men, their economic and cultural and racial groupings. Catholicism by its very objectivity has often shown a greater power to bring together into the presence of the Holy both rich and poor, learned and unlearned, black and white. Catholicism does not characteristically expect them to be friends or to have any marked measure of social intercourse, but it does expect them to come together into God's house. It may be said that the churches of our third type are seeking something harder and higher, but the failure to achieve it may result in something worse.

The fellowships of the Spirit are clearly in their origins the products of enthusiasm. They have issued typically from the creative influence of men deeply moved from within. But enthusiasm is difficult to maintain. Its deposit readily becomes a law for succeeding generations to follow. The profoundly converted man awakens and guides others to an experience convincingly like his own. The converts form an intimate fellowship of shared experience. Then the characteristic language of their testimony becomes a pattern for those to follow who would join this fellowship. The temptation then lies close at hand to make pretensions to a more mature experience than one has truly had. Or a movement which started as an effort to be rid of formulas, develops its own formula without recognizing it for what it is.

The movements of the Spirit easily fall into the error of thinking that what comes to men from within is more independent of that which comes to them from without than it is in fact. Within a man gifted with a rich and active interior life, powerful convictions and impulsions germinate below the levels of deliberate thought. They come to him as simply "given." He shares them and calls upon others to turn within, to listen and to wait and to share what the Spirit gives them. The idea can readily come to them that this experience is entirely unmediated, that they have it without any dependence on what a great society or a great tradition, or their leader, has brought them from beyond themselves. It was Baron von Hügel, I believe, who once observed that the utterances of George Fox showed an extraordinary likeness to the Gospel of John. This is not to minimize in the least the creative originality of George Fox or to question that the Spirit of God worked mightily through him. In him the seed of the Word truly took deep root and brought forth fruit. But the Spirit is not found without the Word, and the Word is carried by the Church.

In an earlier chapter of this book it was observed that each of the divided churches naturally conceives of the unity which should mark the Church in terms of its own form and experience. When a church dreams of the Church to come, it tends to project its own image. This is not simply an expression of ecclesiastical egotism, though it is often that in large measure. It is not simply the result of a habit of mind. The several ideas of the unity which should be sought are part and parcel of the Church ideas out of which they come. No church can dispense with the idea of unity, for it is inseparable from the idea of Church, but there are important differences as to where the unity is to be located, how manifested and how guaranteed.

The ultimate ground of unity is, of course, in God himself; the unity of God's people is to be found only in him. Catholicism has sought *church unity* uncompromisingly because the Church itself as objective institution is seen as the this-world agency, representative and sacrament of God's own unity. The one God cannot be served and represented by divided, conflicting, competing agencies or representatives. The Church as a sacramental society must be the outward and visible sign of the one Kingdom which is in heaven and which is to come. Visible, institutional fragmentation and competition are incongruous with its sacramental meanings; as incongruous as dirty water would be with the sacramental meaning of baptism.

Classical Protestantism has sought *unity in the Word*, in the Book which enshrines the Word, in the confession which interprets the Word, and in the sacraments in which the Word is made visible and sealed. The churches of this inheritance largely lost the realization of the sacramental character of the Church's own visible form. Their forefathers trusted that fidelity to the Book would guarantee the unity of the trustees to whom the Book was committed. But the trustee-churches failed to create any overarching authority strong enough to hold them in fully responsible relations with one another across distance and political obstacles. They had no great will to do so, having just won their freedom at great cost from papal authority; so the broken communities of classical Protestantism developed their own traditions of interpretation, without recognizing clearly the inescapable part played by the living community in the constant reworking of its own inheritance. Where, as in original Calvinism, the outlines of a God-ordained church order were found in the Bible, these churches sought to embody that order in their forms of ministry and of government. Within Lutheranism the surest bond of unity has been found in the confessions, which formulate the truths of God's Word as these churches interpret them.

Time and mutual contact have widely softened the sharp edges of these divergent traditions of interpretation. The churches which are the heirs of these traditions are increasingly aware of a deep kinship. They are prepared by their inheritance to seek for a unity in which the truths of the Reformation are guarded. For they view the Church in its corporate wholeness as the trustee of God's Word and sacraments.

Those who think of the Church predominantly in terms of the fellowship of the Spirit approach the problems of unity with misgivings quite unknown to Catholicism and far less characteristic of classical Protestantism. This applies both to the small and intimate movements among whom the Friends are a kind of spiritual aristocracy, and to the great communions which largely share this third idea of the Church. They are all disposed to say that unity is not to be sought or found in any statement of common faith, in church organization, in a ministry bearing the authority of the whole Church, or in any rites in which all participate. Unity is to be found rather in a consciously shared *inner life.* They speak much of "fellowship." They urge that realized fellowship must always come before what they are inclined to call "a mere organizational unity."

Faced with a choice between order and freedom, their vote will be for freedom. Their tradition is "congregational" and "separatist." They are suspicious of officers and of centralized authority, of church law and of church government. When they grow large and take on tasks and responsibilities as "denominations," they find themselves driven to create superintendents and secretaries and boards. But these tend to be viewed as somewhat unfortunate practical necessities rather than as God's gifts to his church for the guarding of its wider unity. Since their own unity as "denominations" takes the form of an association of free congregations, they naturally turn to that pattern as their model when they seek a more inclusive unity.

The divided heirs of classical Protestantism and the churches of the more radical Protestant type all find themselves faced with common enemies. A godless secularism is taking possession of the cultures within which they live and infiltrating their own membership. They are fearful, often resentful, often unworthily jealous of a Roman Catholicism, militant, effectively united and better disciplined than the sons of the Reformation.

These churches know that they are faced with common tasks in the proclamation of their gospel, in the education of their children, in their public relations and in the dealings with increasingly pervasive governments. The will for unity is growing among them. They consult and confer and work together fitfully in many areas. They associate and federate cautiously. But in their shared background there is a violent reaction against the corruption and the totalitarian claims of Western Catholicism, so violent that it has left them fearful of all overarching church order. Could it be that there are great truths and institutions which they might recover from Catholicism without losing the precious values they carry in their own inheritance?

CHAPTER VII

Prospecting for a United Church

How much easier it is to analyze, however imperfectly, some of the elements in a major human problem than to forecast the lines for its solution! Popular folklore seeks to teach us early that when Humpty Dumpty has once fallen off the wall, the task of putting him together again is too much for all the king's horses and all the king's men. A sweep of the hand can turn to fragments the jigsaw puzzle which it may take hours to form again. The Church and churches are far more easily broken than mended. And plainly we are not here dealing with the flat, fixed, lifeless pieces of a picture whose parts could be fitted back into a whole, the pattern of which we know or can imagine. We are dealing with the living stuff, with millions of human lives, with passions, prejudices, convictions, habits, memories, hopes.

These multitudes of lives are gathered, with many degrees of inner coherence, into great groupings and sub-groupings; they have acquired in the course of their history a stubborn individuality, as our personal lives acquire unique individuality in our private histories. We strive to classify them, but they escape our classifications. There moves in them all an elemental will to live; they struggle for existence. Congregations struggle for existence; denominations struggle for existence; church families struggle for existence. Much of their energy goes into that struggle. They do not want to die. We are like that; we do not want to die unless we can be persuaded that to die would be to enter into a larger life. And how hard it is to be persuaded of that!

94

We have said that we would be as men without hope if there were not moving through the many churches a will for unity which we truly believe to be a reflection of the will of God. We have recognized that the task of any who would serve this cause must be to feed this aspiration and to clarify its goals. Without the will for unity there can be no progress, but the will cannot live and move unless the mind and imagination reach out ahead to point the ways in which it should seek to move.

No one can come to this task without underlying assumptions, and each of us must try to uncover his own assumptions that he and others may examine them. Let us remind ourselves of some of the assumptions that have been developed in this discussion. They have much to do with the approach we make to the problems of a united Church.

The Church consists of human persons knit together in relations with one another and with God coming to men redemptively in Christ. It is a special form of community, a shared life. The distinctive mark of this community is that God in Christ is party to it and is its center. It took its origin when Christ entered our human world and men answered to him and gathered around him. Being knit to him, they were knit to all who were his. Some of us as children played with a magnet and iron filings. We placed the iron filings on a piece of paper and moved the magnet into a position beneath them. Then the iron filings within reach of the magnet took a new orientation and formed a pattern together. That is a very simple picture of the Church in its most elemental nature: a bundle of lives drawn together around Christ, oriented toward him, given their direction by him.

That which is uniquely shared here is the personal relationship with Christ. And since Christ is in intimate filial relation with the Father, ever pointing beyond and above himself to the Father, and since he communicates to those who gather around him in answering loyalty a new Spirit of fellowship, this community is in personal relations with the Father through Christ and in the Spirit.

The Church as a form of human community requires both body

and spirit for its existence. In this respect it is fully analogous to a family or a people. We can assuredly say that it has never been without a body; and that body has certainly developed in response to changing occasions and needs.

We come next to a very crucial assumption underlying this discussion. The assumption is that while the bodily, institutional structure and organs of the Church, on the one hand, and its interior spiritual life, on the other hand, belong together, they have not as fixed a relationship as has commonly been claimed in the debates of history. Community with others in Christ may, and does, survive the loss of precious bodily elements. A church, like a people or like an individual man, may live with a marred and broken body, though not without any body at all. When in the tragic conflicts and accidents of history the body of the Church was broken, each side commonly sought to prove that it was unquestionably the real and true Church. Commonly each sought to unchurch the other. And, as in splittings in a political society, each claimed legitimacy and sought to establish it by some recognizable marks of continuity.

This is not to suggest that in these breaks in the Church's body truth and error were irrelevant. But in the heat of conflict, group egotism usually sought to prove too much and then found itself committed to that too much. In the light of subsequent history and less heated consideration, it appears that the body was indeed broken and marred, but that in the broken fragments enough was left for a very real continuance of shared life in Christ. To change the figure and to use a phrase of Bishop Brent's, "Christ's agile feet journey to the human heart along many and diverse paths."

This is not to say that it does not matter that the body of the Church is broken. It matters greatly. Because the body is broken, life in community as between those of the severed parts is made well-nigh impossible, or is sore let and hindered. Some parts are more fully equipped or differently equipped than others to nurture and guard this life in communion with Christ at its fullest. Yet there is a deep kinship between the sundered fragments so long as there is that in them through which Christ can reach men and gather them around himself. Wherever two or three are gathered in his name, Christ is there; and where he is, there is the Church.

All this is widely, though not universally, recognized in terms of what is often called a "spiritual unity" which exists across and beneath our divisions. It is what makes possible convincing experiences of fellowship between individuals coming out of widely separated churches. But that does not mean that we have no problems to solve; the body is broken and we have the task of recovering or, better, of receiving from God a body that can hold together in rich and realized community the whole people of God.

Recognition of deep kinship must come before reconciliation and healing can begin. A chief obstacle to the recognition of the Church in fragmentized, broken forms arises from the persistent tendency to identify the Church with some outward form—form of words or acts or order or structure of government. This tendency is greatly stiffened by another factor to which reference was made in a previous chapter. The outward elements which form the visible and readily recognized body of a church are seen as the shared possession of God and men. They are means of communion or of communication between God and his people. What man acknowledges to be God's or of God—the bearer of his word, the instruments of his action, the order through which he deals with men and through which men may deal with him—all these take on in their thought and feeling the qualities of God. These things are holy, sacrosanct, charged with mysterious power, not given over to change and decay, immutable.

As a result, there arises a massive obstacle to reconciliation between divided bodies of Christians. It is the tendency to treat as an utterly indispensable *absolute*, or to divinize extravagantly and uncritically, some one element in the body of the Church's life. A particular form of ministry, a particular creed or confession of faith, a particular ordinance or sacramental action, the whole body of canonical Scriptures or some combination of these, is viewed as let down from heaven. As such it is held to be inerrant, utterly indispensable, not partaking of the relativity of human history. God himself is viewed as committed to one or other of these things to such an extent that he will not assuredly be present to men or grant men his blessings save when this formula is used or this action is performed or this official is present.

For one or other of these distinguishable elements claims have been made which many serious and devout Christians find to be contradicted by convincing experience in several ways. The presence of one or other of these particular forms does not appear to guarantee the fruits of the Spirit. These forms show themselves to be corruptible in history. Impressive evidences of the Spirit are found apart from the presence of this one or that one. Honest historians testify that every one of these tangible elements in the life of the Church has grown and changed in form, and certainly in meaning to men of different times. Only God is unchanging. Everything in which man has a hand is subject to change and is relative to him in his time and place.

How readily one may be misunderstood at this point! The thought is not that God has not, indeed, used these many means to reach out to men and to draw them to himself in Christ. The positive claims that blessings are veritably to be found here are generally true. It is the exclusive claims, and the denials that he is the Lord of all means and that he can and does use other means, which are challenged.

Certainly our thought is not that the Church does not need these outward and visible elements for its continuance in health and wholeness. Quite the contrary! The Church is lamed and impoverished without them. But the excessive claims made in the heat of conflict for particular elements in the Church's embodiment become a barrier to the recognition of their value and significance. They might be persuasively commended if less extravagant claims were made for them. A more consistent recognition that everything in which man has a part partakes of man's fallibility and is open to corruption could guard us here.

The excessive claims for the Church's institutional forms within

various types of Catholicism helped to prepare for the disillusionment of man with the institution. The excessive claims for the
Bible in Protestant biblicism served to deepen man's disillusionment
with the Bible when scientific and historical criticism turned that
way. The extravagance of both Catholic and Protestant orthodoxy
in well-nigh identifying the formulations of the faith with God
himself helped to prepare the way for the violent reaction against
all positive doctrines from which many are seeking now to recover.
The destructive violence of those who tore the Church's fabric
apart was in large measure induced by the pretensions of those
who were the guardians of that fabric.

Many sections of the divided Christian community are suffering
from the reckless destruction of that fabric. They try desperately
to keep going by glad-handing, by headlines on church billboards
or by pulpit stunts and sentimentally concocted ceremonies, in
the absence of any majestic body of ordered faith, any ordered
ministry, any deep and meaningful tradition of worship, or any
disciplined way of life such as could feed and steady and illumine
spiritually starved and confused people.

Excessive claims call forth excessive denials. And then both
parties are wont to entrench themselves in hopelessly hostile posi-
tions and it becomes a part of loyalty to one's fathers to hold that
position against all comers. At least this is plainly true, that we shall
not move towards a more united Church if each divided part of
the total Christian community simply projects into the future the
lines of its own ecclesiastical past. The vociferous reiteration of
what are in important measure the products of past conflicts will
not lead to peace and reconciliation. That can come only if there
is recognition of important elements of truth and value in the
witness and the inheritance of those divided from us, and recognition of the overstatement or the neglect of some significant truths
and values in our own history. That is the way reconciliation comes
in personal relationships, and I see no reason to suppose that it
will come otherwise among sections of the Christian community.

Of course, if it is our settled conviction that our own church must always have been infallibly right and, as the saying goes, "has everything," then there is no hope save in the penitent return of the prodigals to our fold. No self-respecting body of Christians is going to enter a union unless the positive values of its tradition and its most sacred memories are taken up and cherished in the new common life, even while its past sins and excesses are forgiven. The power to forgive between man and man or between church and church is given only to those who have known their own need of forgiveness. The ability to accept the limitation of others is present only in those who have gained the self-knowledge which can recognize their own limitations. It is a measure of the reconciliation between north and south in our own nation that they can now begin to treasure together the memories of Lincoln and Lee.

As Richard Niebuhr has written: "We cannot become integrated parts of one common church until we each remember our whole past, with its sins, through Jesus Christ, and appropriate each other's pasts. There will be no union of Catholics and Protestants until through the common memory of Jesus Christ the former repent of the sin of Peter and the latter of the sin of Luther; until Protestants acknowledge Thomas Aquinas as one of their fathers, the Inquisition as their own sin and Ignatius Loyola as one of their own reformers; until Catholics have canonized Luther and Calvin, done repentance for Protestant nationalism, and appropriated Schleiermacher and Barth as their theologians . . . The adoption of John Wesley into their own history by Anglicans, of Calvin and Zwingli by Lutherans, of Fox and Woolman by orthodox Protestants, is not only a necessary prelude to union: it is union . . . [Jesus Christ] reveals the faith and the sin of all the fathers of all the churches; through him we can repent of our fathers' sins and gratefully adopt as our own the faithful, sinful fathers of those from whom we are now separated."[1]

We shall not attempt to offer here what might be called even a sketch of a united Church. Such attempts have been made for

---

[1] H. Richard Niebuhr, *The Meaning of Revelation* (New York: The Macmillan Co., 1941), pp. 119-20.

particular areas and with reference to particular groupings of existing churches. They must continue to be made. We shall attempt rather to suggest some of the truths and values which must be taken up into a united Church. The task is somewhat like the first stages in planning a house. We must first decide what we want included and what we are prepared to exclude. For we are thinking together about a roomier house for God's family.

Even to propose preliminary specifications here is highly presumptuous. Who can pretend to stand in magisterial detachment and to pass judgment on what is right and what is wrong, what is good and abiding or false or dangerous, in major expressions of that movement in history of which Christ is the source and center? But one must take that risk in the hope of being constructively provocative.

It is our thesis that the "Great Church," to use a phrase of my colleague Canon Wedel,[2] must include some strong Catholic elements; equally, the Great Church must embody an evangelical, reformed and constantly reformable Catholicism by including within itself major elements of what we have called classical Protestantism; and it must make room in its household for the recurrent movements of the free Spirit, even if that involves the awkward device of providing in law for conscientious objections to the normal requirements of the law.

When we sit down to list some of the specifications for a united Church which shall be indeed the Great Church, there are a number of truths and values which an appreciative examination of Catholicism, or of the churchly type, will lead us to reckon with very seriously.

One is the indispensability of the social, corporate medium within which the precious reality of personal religious life is nurtured. Prophets and saints and run-of-the-mine devout souls do not arise out of nothing. They arise out of a culture, and that culture is carried in a living, embodied community. Because Christ was a

[2] Theodore O. Wedel, *The Coming Great Church* (New York: The Macmillan Co., 1945).

historical event, though recognized by faith as more than that, the continuing possibility of relations with him is made available only within the continuing community issuing from his impact on history. Only within that community are his image, his words, the sacramental extension of his own action, his presence, borne. He continues to work redemptively in history through the continuity of the community of memory and of hope rooted in him. The faith that he is Lord of history carries with it inevitably the derivative faith that the gates of hell shall not prevail against his Church. If his Church ceased to be, he would become as one who had not been, so far as our ongoing life in this world is concerned. Continuity with its own origins and its own past is of the essence of the Church. The Catholic concern with continuity, and with that which guards and symbolizes continuity, is crucial for the Church.

Tradition, the living process by which a community constantly transmits, interprets and reinterprets its own inheritance, is not eliminated by being anathematized. What the Bible or the ancient revelatory events and persons of which it speaks mean to men is always shaped by the living culture or community of thought and life within which the Bible comes to men. Even its language becomes dead language to men standing within a culture in which its terms or imagery no longer possess living meaning. That is just where multitudes of our contemporaries now stand. Protestantism does not escape the interpretative process of tradition by refusing to look at it. The Bible ceases to speak to men when separated from the living Church.

Catholicism can teach us the value of forms, conventions if you will; that they can be means of grace—forms of prayer, forms of worshiping act, forms of church architecture, forms of ministry. Surely we recognize that social forms, even manners, are means of grace on the plane of human social relations. There is no escaping form, and when we try to do so we usually find ourselves using impoverished forms. If, to use Professor Lowes' phraseology, "convention and revolt" are an inescapable part of the ongoing life of

poetry, are they not an inescapable part of the art of communal
life in Christ?

Catholicism can teach us, if we are not too stubborn or fearful
to learn, the power of the bodily act, the effectual place of the
outward and visible and tangible in the nurture and fulfillment of
spiritual community or communion. I meet a stranger on a train.
We talk together, and finally we shake hands. That is the climax
of our meeting; the word blossoms to fulfillment in the act. So
for Catholicism, Christ in his Church takes children into his arms
to bless, and his broken body is offered to and for men. There are
dangers here, dangers to be guarded against; but shall we handle
nothing in life that is dangerous?

Catholicism can teach us that the Great Church, like a great
people, cannot maintain vigorous community across space and
across the years and across human differences without a body of
comparable dimensions. It requires means of intercommunication
and of responsible common council. It needs shared forms: forms
of words which in spite of changing meaning and diversity of
interpretation catch and reinforce as well as words can the animating faith of the great community. It needs ways of holding and
renewing its shared memories and refreshing its communion with
the springs of its own life. It needs shared symbols and acts which
all can recognize as embodying its most central devotion. It is
greatly helped, to put the matter no more strongly, by personages
who are not simply competent technicians in the machinery of its
affairs, office men, but who are given a symbolic and in a broad
sense a sacramental character. In their own unworthy persons they
serve as binders across the barriers of localism and as guardians of
continuity, even as bearers of the potencies carried in the life of
the Church itself. Perhaps the reader will recognize bishops
beneath this veil of words. Such personages have proved dangerous
in history and have been known to develop a dangerous will to
power and to manifest delusions of grandeur. Well then, surround
them with constitutional checks and balances; but do not fail to

consider them seriously if you seek a Great Church and a ministry which can be clearly recognized throughout it as representative of its whole continuing common life.

That gifted and valiant gadfly in our American Protestant world, Dr. Charles Clayton Morrison, has written recently of the ineffectualness of a fragmentized church in dealing with the powerful magnitudes of our contemporary world, such as secularized education, the radio, the movies, organized labor, or government. Individuals can deal best with individuals. Little local fellowships can reach out most fruitfully into the intimacies of family life and neighborhood. But only strong social magnitudes can wrestle on anything like equal terms with other social magnitudes. In our capital city of Washington, where justice and law are architecturally embodied in a Supreme Court building, and the presidency in a White House, and the treasured memories of this people in a Washington Monument and a Lincoln Memorial, only a majestic Cathedral can put the Church in the social scene in comparable terms. The architecture of a Great Church must be equal to its greatness, and not simply in the primary meaning of architecture, but in its total structure. A world Church requires a world structure visible to men.

We cannot simply concoct these structures or create them by legislative action. They must develop out of and gather meaning in life in community. When they have been lost, they have to be recovered from history. That does not mean that they are subject to no modification; in history, they are always undergoing modification and reinterpretation.

All these elements which we have proposed for inclusion in any specifications for a united Church have proved dangerous in history, not least a Great Church itself. They need to be counterweighted, checked, held in dynamic equilibrium with other elements. That brings us to the elements which classical Protestantism must feed into a united Church if it is to embody evangelical, reformed and constantly reformable Catholicism, salted with that which alone can save Catholicism from corruption. Some of us think that we know the forms of that corruption, the sicknesses and perils of an uncriticized Catholicism; divinization of the hierarchical church, dangerous centralization of power, pretensions of infallibility, stiff, unyielding traditionalism, externalism, legalism, traffic in holy substances, holy medals, holy formulas, which verges on primitive magic. Perhaps this is an ungenerous and prejudiced judgment. Then let those of Catholic inheritance who are sensitive to these dangers teach us where we are wrong.

As we have seen, classical Protestantism represents in its several expressions a powerful reassertion of God's sovereignty and transcendence with respect to his Church. It witnesses to the permanently normative position of the originative Word, which means above all the Word made flesh and witnessed to in the Gospels. Christ, the Christ of the Gospels, is forever the Lord of the Church. Men are to be confronted with him and summoned to answer to him. That is the sovereign encounter of their lives. Their response to him and their standing in his sight can never be unqualifiedly identified with their response to any actual embodiment of his Church. A man's acceptability to any church authorities, clerical or lay, cannot *guarantee* his acceptability before Christ, nor can a man's unacceptability to them establish without question his unacceptability before Christ. No church personages or hierarchy of personages can present themselves unqualifiedly as his agents. They must always point beyond themselves to him and leave men in face-to-face encounter with him, not tenaciously intruding themselves as though God in Christ and his people could converse only through an interpreter or have deep dealings only through a go-between.

That does not mean that the Church's ministry cannot proclaim the gospel with authority and declare with authority Christ's forgiveness toward the penitent and assure men as to where God in Christ is veritably to be met with. He is to be met with in the Gospels and in the sacramental, embodied fellowship of the faithful, supremely when the fellowship bows in penitent, grateful adoration before the enacted memorial and re-presentation of the offered life of its Lord, and reaches out to take to itself the meaning and power of his broken and victorious life. The Church and the Church's ordained agents cannot manage that meeting. They can only offer it and prepare the way for it. Christ must be discerned within the Gospels by the inward testimony of the Spirit, and received in the sacrament by faith.

Classical Protestantism knows that the Church is not infallible or incorruptible. God in Christ creates and must constantly re-create his Church. Its members do not stand in intellectual or moral bondage to any hierarchy or priesthood; they are to be constantly referred back beyond the given church to the Lord, and summoned to make their responsible answers as free men to him.

Classical Protestantism sought to guard and institutionalize its witness by making the gospel, and more generally the Bible in which the gospel is set, directly available to the humblest member of the Church, and by establishing the preached word firmly along-side the Church's sacramental action. That means that the member-ship of the Church is constantly offered its own direct access to the primitive, normative self-disclosure of God. It means that the ministry is constantly charged to go directly to the record of the Word made flesh, to the prophetic Word and to the apostolic Word, and open that Word to the contemporary Church in contemporary language.

This is the most effective guard which is offered against the corruption of sacramentalism as unchecked by the ministry of the Word. In human community or social relations, the uttered word is the best medium of intelligible and moral fellowship. The touch of the hand or the meeting of the lips provides intimacy and seals and strengthens fellowship, but without the word, the intimacy, the moving, binding intimacy of contact, lacks intelligible meaning and moral content. So it is in men's shared community or com-munion with God in Christ. Sacraments are the parallels in religious relationship to the communicative, strengthening realism of bodily presence and the direct touch of life with life in the deepest social relationships. Where they are lacking or neglected or where their meaning is thinned, men are likely to be left with the impression that they have had many messages from God but have not come into his very Presence. Surely part of the manifest drawing power of Catholic sacramentalism is the assurance it brings to common men that they have come into the real Presence.

The Great Church must embody in its life the witness of classical Protestantism to the open, accessible Bible, and the constant resubmission of its ongoing life to the Word which comes to it from God out of the primitive witness.

The Bible is not verbally inspired or literally inerrant. To divinize the Book is as false as to divinize the visible Church, for man had his large part in the making of the Book as in the making of the Church. The Bible offers no guarantee of unity in itself, for as modern scholarship indubitably shows it possesses no simple unity. The Great Church needs Catholic order to guard its unity across space and across time, even as it needs the open Book and the Spirit-illumined preaching of the Word to guard that order from corruption. The Bible requires continual reinterpretation by the living community, but it is the Bible and supremely Christ in the Bible that requires this continual reinterpretation.

We are wrestling with the specifications for the Great Church. For its order, its visible architectural unity, and for the guarding of its continuity with its own past, we turn to that broad type of community in Christ which we have designated as the Catholic type. For its preservation against corruption, to keep it true to its unique origin, to be sure that in its building and constant rebuilding it remains rightly centered, we must turn to the contributions of classical Protestantism and to the foundation other than which no man can lay.

What of that third way of conceiving and embodying community in Christ, whose many variants we have tried to gather up under the terms "the fellowship of the Spirit" or "the community of the perfect way"? Have these nothing to bring to the specifications for the Great Church? Assuredly, yes!

The Church desperately needs the Spirit and must provide in its life for constant openness to that free, spontaneous, creative Spirit who is not always the Comforter but often the Disturber. The Spirit has shaped and indwelt many forms in the long life of the Christian community. But there is no form or institution from which the Spirit may not depart, leaving it standing as a lifeless shell given over to decay. The Spirit is most unmistakably present and creative in the intimate fellowship of little human companies gathered about Christ and sharing his meaning for them in the give and take of face-to-face sharing. These fellowships in their many expressions can teach us many things and bring to us precious values out of their treasury of experience.

They manifest the unique values and powers of the little church within the Great Church. Many of us who live within relatively formalized communions can testify to the distinctive quality of the little, simple, local church, rooted in neighborhood, with its church suppers and its homey, family quality. We can testify to the renewal which has come to us in little groups meeting for the sharing of spontaneous prayer and common concerns. It is as contrary to experience to deny that Christ finds men and is found of men in these simple ways as it is to deny that he comes among men in the sacraments of his Church. The affirmations men make in faith are commonly true, when they declare that here or there Christ has found them. It is their exclusive claims and their denials which are more commonly false. The long debate between liturgy and spontaneous, extempore prayer, ends in a fruitless stalemate. Liturgical prayers have values which are obvious to the unprejudiced and discerning, but free prayer possesses an immediacy, a concreteness, a direct relevance to life which liturgy cannot provide. A church in which lay men and women never share the stumbling prayers of their own ecclesiastically nonprofessional hearts is impoverished. The simple observances of the Lord's Supper embody and communicate what is readily obscured in the more ornate and formalized celebration of the Holy Communion or the Eucharist, and vice versa. It is true that the people of God are called to be "friends" and "brethren" in their relations one with another, and the little companies in which this is realized are centers of renewal in the Great Church, if only they can keep free from the self-righteousness which ever threatens those who seek earnestly the perfect way.

If we ask ourselves, "How does one provide for the Spirit in the Church?," the answer is not easy. The Spirit refuses to be fully institutionalized or domesticated; the Spirit cannot be brought under law or bound by the Book. He bloweth where he listeth. We can only wait for the Spirit. We cannot produce the Spirit; most direct efforts to produce the Spirit or fellowship in the Spirit end in frustrated weariness. What we can do is to have waiting places and waiting times in the Church, unregulated areas in its structure, open spaces and some wide-open doors.

We have been speaking of the specifications for a united Church. If the firm of consulting ecclesiastical architects to whom we presented these were to shake their heads and ask, "Do you really expect to get all that under one roof?," we would have to say, "We do not know about the one roof." Perhaps we should dream, rather, in terms of a "center," to use a contemporary architectural term; a central structure with other structures gathered around it, all forming a unity and with the internal channels of communication wide open. Or, to use political language, perhaps we should think in federal terms.

Ultimately God in history must be the Architect and the Builder, and we only subcontractors. But surely since God must build his Great Church through embodied human minds and hearts it will make all the difference what we greatly will to have included. So we must go on wrestling together about the truths and values to be included. As we come together out of our many traditions, some will say, "Church, Bible, Spirit; but the greatest of these is Spirit." Others will say, "Church, Spirit, Bible; but the greatest of these is Bible." Still others, "Bible, Spirit, Church; but the greatest of these is Church." We are sure that Church, Scripture, the living experience of the Spirit, cannot be put asunder where God has joined them together.

Blessed shall we be if, coming before God together, we can say: "We come before Thee, O God, bearing the manifold gifts Thou hast given. Take these Thy gifts and us who are the bearers of them; and grant that being no more strangers and foreigners to one another, but fellow citizens with the saints and with the household of God, we may be built upon the foundation of the apostles and prophets, Jesus Christ himself being the chief cornerstone; in whom all the building fitly framed together may grow into a holy temple acceptable unto Thee."

INDEX

Anabaptists, 18
Anglicanism, 24, 29, 58
Anglo-catholicism, 47, 58-59
Augustine, 72

Baptists, 18, 29, 77
Bible
  availability of, to all, 106
  as basis of classical Protestant idea
    of the Church, 47, 60-74
  continual reinterpretation of, 107
  different interpretations of, 69-71
  divinized, 107
  position of, in "Great Church,"
    104-107
  as supreme "rule of faith," 83
Bodily act, power of, 103
Brent, Bishop Charles Henry,
    quoted, 22, 96
Brotherliness, 89

Calvin, John, 18, 69-70, 72, 74
Calvinism, 91
Canada, United Church of, 25, 27
Catholicism. *See also* Eastern Orth-
    odoxy *and* Roman Catholicism
  activity and presence of God in,
    51, 53-54
  Anglican version of, 59
  concept of the Church held by,
    46-47, 48-59
  division of, into Eastern and
    Western, 17

elements of, to be embodied in
    the "Great Church," 101, 102-
    105
  emphasis of, on "the faith," 51,
    73, 83
  as the great society, 46
  impersonality of, 76
  infallibility of, 51
  intolerance in, 57
  laity in, 54
  legalism in, 56
  man dependent on society in,
    50
  "mixed" character of, 56, 72, 78
  as partaking of quality of God, 51
  priesthood in, 53-54, 68, 86
  Roman and Orthodox, compared,
    57-58
  sacraments in, 52
  as spiritual ancestor of Protestant-
    ism, 49
  traditionalism in, 55
  unity and universality in, 18, 89
  use of word "catholic," 46-47
  as a visible, continuing institu-
    tion, 50
  worship in, 53, 55, 84
Charity, 11, 46
Christ
  continual reinterpretation of, 107
  duality of, 40
  embodiment of community in,
    107-108

faith in, as Lord of history, 102
as Lord of the Church, 105
personal relationship with, 95
as revelation of God's love, 62
Church, the. *See also* "Great Church"
American contribution to denominationalism in, 19
bodily and spiritual aspects of, 96
Catholic view of, 46-47, 48-59
classical Protestant idea of, 47, 60-74
differing concepts of, 13-15, 46-93
as fellowship of the Spirit (or community of the Perfect Way), 47-48, 75-93
as a form of community, 95, 96
fragmentation of, 7-8, 18-19
idea of, in churches of the Spirit, 47-48, 75-93
influence of various ideas of, 44-45
"three-branch theory" of, 15
three broad concepts of, 46-49
undivided, period of, 17
as world fellowship, 25
Church of England, 70
Churches
analogy of, to "family" and "people," 32-37, 38-39
bodily and spiritual aspects of, 30, 36-42
changes of allegiance to, 2
and the Church, incongruity between, 13-14
common origin and inheritance of, 9-10
community, 21-22
confession of the Church by, 8-9, 10-11
cooperation among, 20-22, 24-25, 26-28
distinguishing traits of, 45
division among, 7-8

economy and efficiency in work of, 21-22
as forms of human association, 36-40
individual experience in, 1-3
influence of varying concepts of the Church on, 44-45
main types of, 6-7
relation of, to others of their kind, 3-4
size and "catholicity" of, 39
social relationship of, with God, 39-41, 42-43
of the Spirit, *see* Spirit, churches of the
as sum total of the Church, 15
tendency of, to divinize elements of church life, 42-43, 97-99
Communion, 67, 85
Community church, 21-22
Community of the Perfect Way, concept of the Church as, 47-48, 75-93
Conference, world, 24-25
Congregation
as the "blessed community," 82
fellowship of, 81-83
"sociable" element in, 81
Congregational churches, 18, 77
Congregationalism, 88, 92
Continuity, as essence of the Church, 102
Conversion, 2, 80
Cooperative relations of churches, 19-22, 24-25, 26-28
Creeds, aversion to, of churches of the Spirit, 83-84

Denominations, 3-6, 18-19; *see also* Churches
differences within, 7
unity within, 9-10
Disciples of Christ, 77

Eastern Orthodoxy, 57
Episcopal system, 70, 102-103

Faith, 79-80
    and "the faith," 51-52, 65-66, 83
    invisibility of, 72, 74
    Protestant emphasis on, 64, 65-
        66, 73-74, 83
Faith and Order (Hodgson, ed.),
    quoted, 12
Family, bodily and spiritual aspects
    of, 32-34
Federal Council of Churches, 24
Federation, cooperative, 26-28
Fellowship
    of the congregation, 81-83
    of the saints, the Church as, 80
    of the Spirit, concept of the
        Church as, 47-48, 75-93
    world, 25
Forms, value of, 102-103
Friends, Religious Society of, 48,
    76, 92

God
    love of, revealed in Christ, 62
    position of, above institutions
        and agencies, 61-62
    presence and activity of, in Cath-
        olic view of the Church, 51,
        53-54
    social relationship of church with,
        39-41, 42-43
Government, as instrument and
    symbol, 36
"Great Church." *See also* Church,
    the
    architecture of, 104
    elements of Catholicism to be
        embodied in, 101, 102-105
    elements of churches of the Spir-
        it to be embodied in, 101, 107-
        109
    elements of classical Protestant-
        ism to be embodied in, 101,
        105-108
    preservation of, against corrup-
        tion, 107

Hooker, Richard, quoted, 71

Human association
    analogy of churches to aspects of,
        29-37
    churches as forms of, 37-40

Intercommunion, 26-27
Interpretation
    of the Bible, 69-71, 107
    of Christ, 107
    traditions of, 84, 91
Intolerance, 57

Kelly, Thomas R., quoted, 82

Laity, Catholic, 54
Leadership, 85
Legalism, 56
Luther, Martin, 18, 69, 72, 73-74
Lutheranism, 18, 24, 29, 47, 60,
    69, 72, 91

Marriage, 31-32
Mass, 53, 81
Meaning of Revelation, The (Nie-
    buhr), quoted, 100
Methodism, 18, 77
Ministry
    Catholic, 53-55, 68, 86
    of churches of the Spirit, 87-88
    of classical Protestantism, 67-69
        86-87
Morrison, Charles Clayton, 104

Nation. *See* People
Nationalism, rise of, 70
Niebuhr, Richard, quoted, 29, 100

Orthodox churches. *See* Eastern
    Orthodoxy

Papacy, 17, 51, 58
People (nation), bodily and spirit-
    ual elements of, 34-37
Personal experience
    and fellowship of the Spirit, 47-
        48, 75, 76
    shared, 89

Presbyterianism, 18, 47, 60

Priesthood. *See* Ministry
  of all believers, 65, 68

Protestantism
  churches of the Spirit within, 47-
    48, 75-93
  fragmentation in, 75-77
  Protestantism, classical, concept of
    the Church in, 15, 47, 60-74
  based on the Bible, 47, 60-74
  definition of, 72
  distinction of inward and out-
    ward aspects of, 72-74
  divisive elements in, 69-72
  elements of, to be embodied in
    the "Great Church," 101, 104-
    107
  as God's love revealed through
    Christ, 62
  ministry, in, 67-68, 86-87
  place of faith in, 65-66, 72, 73-
    74, 83
  position of God above institutions
    and agencies in, 61-62
  priesthood of all believers in, 65,
    68
  sacraments in, 66-67
  tradition in, 76

Reformation, 18, 47, 60-64, 69-70
  corruption preceding, 61

Religious Society of Friends. *See*
  Friends, Religious Society of

Roman Catholicism. *See also* Catholicism
  compared to Eastern Orthodoxy,
    57
  condemnation of Protestantism
    by, 57-58
  as the one true Church, 14, 29
  and Protestantism, chasm be-
    tween, 26

Sacraments
  Catholic, 52
  of churches of the Spirit, 85

of classical Protestantism, 66-67

Saints, the Church as fellowship of,
  80

Separatism, 92-93

Social experience, common ground
  in, 30-31

South India, United Church of, 25,
  27

Spirit, churches of the
  aversion of, to "human creeds,"
    83-84
  congregationalism in, 88, 92
  elements of, to be embodied in
    the "Great Church," 101, 107-
    109
  enthusiasm of, 89
  fellowship within, 81-82
  ministry in, 86-87
  personal character of, 47-48, 75,
    76, 88-89
  sacraments in, 85
  traditions of interpretation in, 84
  unity of, in shared inner life,
    92-93
  worship in, 84-85

Spirit. *See also* Churches, bodily
    and spiritual aspects of fam-
    ily, 33-34
  fellowship of, as idea of the
    Church, 47-48, 75-93
  of a people, 35-37

Student Christian Movement, 21

Temple, Archbishop, quoted, 11, 12

Testament of Devotion, A (Kelly),
  quoted, 82

"Three-branch theory" of the
  Church, 15

Tradition
  Catholic, 55
  in the Church, 102
  of interpretation, 84, 91

Unitarianism, 18

United Church of Canada, 25, 27

United Church of South India,
  25, 27

Unity
  based in God, 90
  call to, from God to man, 22
  Catholic idea of, 90-91
  within Catholicism, 17-18, 56-57
  of the Church, 11-12
  within denominations, 9-10
  dependence of, on recognition of kinship, 97
  differences within, 7
  half measures toward, 26
  historical struggle for, 16-17
  motives for, 21-23
  obstacles to, 28, 97-99
  problems of, 99-100
  recent progress toward, 24-26
  reviving will to, 19-21
  as shared inner life, 92-93
  spiritual, 97
  truths and values necessary to, 100-110
  in the Word, 91
Wholeness, need for, 23
Word of God. See Bible
World Council of Churches, 24
Worship
  Catholic, 53, 55, 84
  in churches of the Spirit, 85
  classical Protestant, 84-85

Young Men's and Young Women's Christian Association, 20